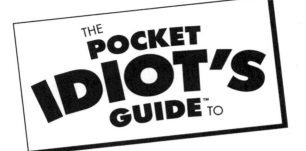

THE
POCKET
IDIOT'S
GUIDE™ TO

Islam

by Jamal J. Elias,
adapted by Nancy D. Lewis

ALPHA

A Pearson Education Company

Adapted from the original, published as *Religions of the World: Islam, First Edition*, by Jamal J. Elias, published by Pearson Education, Inc., publishing as Prentice Hall, Copyright © 1999 Laurence King Publishing Ltd.

The Pocket Idiot's Guide to Islam published by Pearson Education, Inc., publishing as Alpha Books, Copyright © 2003, Laurence King Publishing Ltd.

International Standard Book Number: 0-02-864483-2
Library of Congress Catalog Card Number: 2002115294

04   03   02   8   7   6   5   4   3   2   1

Interpretation of the printing code: The rightmost number of the first series of numbers is the year of the book's printing; the rightmost number of the second series of numbers is the number of the book's printing. For example, a printing code of 02-1 shows that the first printing occurred in 2002.

Printed in the United States of America

Note: This publication contains the opinions and ideas of its author. It is intended to provide helpful and informative material on the subject matter covered. It is sold with the understanding that the author and publisher are not engaged in rendering professional services in the book. If the reader requires personal assistance or advice, a competent professional should be consulted.

The author and publisher specifically disclaim any responsibility for any liability, loss, or risk, personal or otherwise, which is incurred as a consequence, directly or indirectly, of the use and application of any of the contents of this book.

For marketing and publicity, please call: 317-581-3722

The publisher offers discounts on this book when ordered in quantity for bulk purchases and special sales.

For sales within the United States, please contact: Corporate and Government Sales, 1-800-382-3419 or corpsales@pearsontechgroup.com

Outside the United States, please contact: International Sales, 317-581-3793 or international@pearsontechgroup.com

Contents

Introduction

Writing a brief introductory book of this kind presents a set of unique challenges that are particularly acute in the case of Islam. It is a religion of people from vastly varying cultures and simultaneously one that is perceived as foreign to the Western world. In the interest of clarity, this book will concentrate on a limited number of societies when providing concrete examples of Islamic beliefs and customs.

Emphasizing Islam as a living tradition, this book focuses on the religion of ordinary Muslims who live in societies that are mostly in a state of relative peace, and whose major concerns revolve around day-to-day issues. The sensational events and controversies of newspaper headlines are intentionally avoided.

Extras

The sidebars in this book offer extra information and help to explain the topics and terms throughout the book. Use these as road signs on the journey to understanding Islam.

On the Right Path

These boxes provide general guidance about Islam, which support the materials in the text. They take a topic one step further toward understanding the religion.

Muslim Meaning

These boxes define terms familiar to Islam that are used in the text. Understanding the typical vocabulary and jargon of the religion helps you to better understand the general subject when you encounter these terms in another context.

Bet You Didn't Know

These boxes are extra tidbits of background information that are informative or just plain interesting.

Trademarks

All terms mentioned in this book that are known to be or are suspected of being trademarks or service marks have been appropriately capitalized. Alpha Books and Pearson Education, Inc., cannot attest to the accuracy of this information. Use of a term in this book should not be regarded as affecting the validity of any trademark or service mark.

Chapter 1

Islam in Life and Society

In This Chapter

- Obedience to Allah
- The Qur'an
- Sacred traditions of Hadith and Sunna
- Venerating Muhammad

The central shared characteristic of all Muslims (followers of the Islamic faith) is their belief in a God (Allah) who sent a verbal revelation called the Qur'an (or Koran) through a human prophet (Muhammad), who was born around 570 C.E. in the Arabian city of Mecca and died in the nearby city of Medina in 632 C.E.

Muhammad is considered the primary prophet of Islam. He is believed by Muslims to have received divine revelation in the form of the Qur'an and to be the last in a series of prophets beginning with Adam and including all the prophets mentioned in the Hebrew Bible, as well as Jesus.

The specific ways in which God's identity, the nature of revelation, and the concept of prophecy are understood have varied over time and in different contexts, but the centrality of these elements in defining Islamic identity has not changed. This chapter will introduce you to these elements and start you on your path to understanding the religion of Islam.

Allah: Stern and Vengeful or Merciful and Compassionate?

God is commonly referred to by his Arabic name Allah, most likely derived from *al-ilah*, literally meaning "The God." He is also frequently called *al-Rabb*, Arabic for "the Lord." He is often also referred to using whatever the generic word for God is in the various languages spoken by Muslims (for example, *Khuda* in Indo-Iranian languages, and *Tanri* or *Tengri* in Turkic ones).

Western scholarship on Islam has sometimes represented the Muslim God as being stern and vengeful, and the relationship of human beings to him as one of servitude largely motivated by fear of punishment and, secondarily, by the desire for sensual rewards in heaven. For many Muslims, however, the overarching characteristics of God are his nurturing mercy and compassion; the ideal attitude that human beings should have toward him is not one of fearful obedience but of gratitude.

On the Right Path

Pious Muslims try to begin every action, from religious ritual to mundane activities such as beginning a journey to the grocery store, with the formula "In the name of God, the Compassionate, the Merciful." This phrase marks the opening of chapters in the Qur'an and has been used to start formal correspondence throughout Islamic history.

Obedience

In the face of God's overwhelming kindness, disobedience to God becomes synonymous with denying his generosity, and evil is therefore the same as ingratitude. Like the Qur'an, many Islamic theological writings see the entire universe as in a state of obedience to God's law; the word *Islam* literally refers to this state of surrender. Human beings are the only creations that have the capacity to disobey, and they do this by arrogantly thinking that they are self-sufficient, not needing God's support or guidance.

Muslim Meaning

Islam literally means "surrender" or "submission," and is the name of a monotheistic religion closely related to Judaism and Christianity; people belonging to this religion are called Muslims.

A commonly repeated Islamic tradition states that God is closer to a person than his or her jugular vein, implying that God permeates the cosmos. Islamic systems of ritual observance assume that there is a wakeful, attentive God who listens to and cares about each and every one of his creations. Throughout the Islamic world, there is a certain newsworthiness to miraculous stories of how the name of God or the Islamic profession of faith appears in the pattern on the sides of a fish, or how the bleat of a particular sheep sounds as if the animal is singing the praises of God. A pigeon's coo sounds like "Him! Him!" in Arabic, and in Pakistan, a partridge cries out "Glory be to your creation!"

Divine Law

Many Muslims see Islam as the submission to divine law, and anything that has surrendered itself to this law as being called Muslim (f. *Muslima*). Religious and pious human beings often prefer the words *muhsin* and *mu'min*, the former term applying to someone who does good deeds, is righteous and beneficent, and the latter to someone who believes or has faith. The word for faith, *iman*, is closely related to the words for safety, security, and trust, and for many Muslims having faith automatically implies being in God's protection, secure within the principles of guidance he has provided. The belief in God's oneness is called *tawhid*, which not only means "divine unity" but also a person's act of affirming that unity. The word for piety *taqwa* also carries connotations of strength and empowerment.

Muslims see their relationship with God as an intimate one in which God's creation of human beings is a blessing, and his laws and restrictions are not an affliction but an act of grace providing guidance in this life. Many Muslims hold the belief that our life in this world is actually a test for an eternal afterlife; God has provided us with clear guidance through scripture and prophets, so if we still choose to disobey him, we deserve whatever forms of unpleasantness await us in the hereafter.

The Qur'an

For many Muslims the Qur'an is the single greatest sign of God in the physical universe. In fact, individual verses of the Qur'an are called *ayat* (literally meaning "signs"). The text refers to itself as "guidance for the world" and "a clear sign for those who can understand." It provides instructions on how to live your life, and it also acts as a source of ethical guidance for the things that it does not provide clear instruction on.

It is a common Muslim belief that, as God's final revelation, the Qur'an contains the sum total of what God plans to reveal to humanity; therefore, behind the finite, literal message of the Qur'an is an infinite reservoir of divine wisdom.

On the Right Path

The word "Qur'an" is derived from the Arabic verb meaning to read or to recite. "Qur'an" therefore means something like a recitation, or a collection of things to be recited. Muslims often refer to their scripture simply as the Qur'an but normally add a title that signifies respect, such as *al-Karim* (the Noble) or *al-Azim* (the Magnificent). Within the Qur'an itself, the term *al-Kitab* (the Book) is used as an alternative.

In the Prophet Muhammad's opinion and that of the majority of pious believers, the Qur'anic revelations came from heaven, where they were preserved on a "well-guarded Tablet," a concealed supernatural book that existed in the presence of God. Muhammad did not become acquainted with the whole of the Qur'an at once, but only with isolated sections of it. The Qur'an contains only a few obscure hints as to how it was communicated to Muhammad. In fact, it is from later Islamic writings (including the *Hadith*) that we learn how Muhammad would occasionally go into trances when he received a revelation and would then recite it to those around him.

Muhammad believed that his prophetic mission (and the revelations of the earlier Hebrew prophets and the holy scriptures of the Jews and Christians) were based on the original heavenly book, so that they coincided in part with what he himself taught. The Qur'an thus confirms what was revealed earlier: the laws that were given to Moses, the Gospel of Jesus, and other prophetic texts.

> **Muslim Meaning**
>
> The **Hadith** contains traditions or anecdotes concerning the life and sayings of the Prophet Muhammad. It is used as a religious source of secondary importance to the Qur'an.

Style of the Qur'an

Although the stories contained in the Qur'an and the concept of revelation through a series of prophets are shared with the Hebrew Bible and the New Testament, the style of the Qur'an is more in keeping with that of the pre-Islamic Arab religious tradition of *seers* and *oracles*. The text is written neither in prose nor poetry, but consists of rhymed prose, which is easier to remember than normal prose but is not as restricted in style as poetry.

> **Muslim Meaning**
>
> A **seer** or **oracle** is a person who predicts the future through rational, intuitive, or magical means.

The text is arranged in 114 chapters called *suras*. These are unequal in length, some being several pages while others are only a few lines. The chapters are not arranged in a way that reflects the order of revelation. In fact, they seem to be in roughly the opposite of chronological order. They appear to be arranged by length, going from the longest to the shortest.

> **Muslim Meaning**
>
> A **sura** is the term used for the individual chapters of the Qur'an.

Suras are traditionally identified by their names rather than by their numbers. These names are normally distinctive or unusual words that appear somewhere in the early part of the sura, for example, the Cow, the Bee, the Fig, Day Break, and the Clatterer. The suras are further subdivided into verses called *ayat*. Twenty-nine of the chapters begin with seemingly disjointed letters that are referred to as the "mysterious letters," which may convey some secret religious meaning, or may just signify a filing system for organizing the Qur'an.

The Qur'an Becomes a Book

The Qur'an was not put together during Muhammad's lifetime but was preserved on whatever material was then available: bits of parchment, leaves, shoulder blades of camels, and in the memory of his followers. After Muhammad's death, people decided to start collecting the works, but the process took several years. Some say that the Qur'an was collected in its present form within two years of his death under the leadership of his friend and first *Caliph*, Abu Bakr (d. 634). Others contend that the Caliph Umar (d. 644) was the first to compile the Qur'an. Vast arguments have raged ever since, concerning issues of theology and early Arab history, over who gathered together the first edition, and what it consisted of.

Muslim Meaning

Caliphs are the leaders of the Muslim community after Muhammad. The term comes from the Arabic word khalifa, which means "representative" or "delegate," implying that the Caliphs did not rule on their own authority but only as the representatives of God and his prophet. Abu Bakr was Muhammad's friend, advisor, father of his wife A'isha, and the first Caliph of the Sunnis (the largest sect within Islam).

Today, however, most agree that the established canon of the Qur'an, the written text Muslims use today, was completed between 650 and 656 C.E., during the reign of Umar's successor, the Caliph Uthman. His commission decided what was to be included and excluded; it also fixed the number and order of the Suras. That said, unofficial versions of the Qur'an were not entirely forgotten, and these were referred to in subsequent histories and commentaries on the Qur'an.

While the spread of the official text of the Qur'an under Uthman was a major step toward uniformity in versions of the scripture, its importance may easily be exaggerated. For one thing, knowledge of the Qur'an among Muslims was based far more on memory than on writing. For another, the early Arabic script of the Qur'an was a sort of shorthand: Only consonants were written, and the same letter shape could indicate more than one sound. This script was simply an aid to memorization; it presupposed that the reader had some familiarity with the text. It was not until the reign of Abd al-Malik (685–705 C.E.) that the modern Arabic script was created, with its vowels and the use of one letter shape for one sound.

Qur'an in Islamic Tradition

Belief in the Qur'an's being God's literal word has had far-reaching implications: There has traditionally been some resistance to the Qur'an's translation from Arabic into other languages. And although this reticence is now largely gone, traditional etiquette still requires that you refer to printed volumes of the Qur'an as *masahif* (singular: *mushaf*, literally meaning "binding" or "volume"), implying that the divine word is singular and cannot be perfectly contained in ink and paper.

Bet You Didn't Know

It is still uncommon for bookstores to write prices on copies of the Qur'an; the appropriate etiquette for a potential purchaser is to ask what the suitable "gift" for the volume should be.

The special status accorded to the Qur'an goes far beyond the semantics of what to call it. To this day there is great prestige in memorizing the text, and one who knows it in its entirety is called *hafiz* (literally "guardian"), an honorific title that hearkens back to a time when the Qur'an was transmitted orally and committing it to memory was to participate in guarding the text from loss or corruption.

Children across the Islamic world, whether they know any Arabic or not, take Qur'an lessons in which they learn the Arabic script and how to sound the words phonetically. Pious Muslims often try to read a thirtieth of the book every night, so that they can finish the Qur'an every month. Those who cannot read simply run their fingers along its lines, believing that they derive merit through this simple act of devotion.

The Qur'an thus becomes simultaneously a source of prayer and a prayer in its own right, a guidebook for action as well as a ritual object. Devout Muslims treat volumes of the Qur'an with great reverence:

They are not shelved with other books in the house but occupy a position of honor, and readers enter a state of ritual purity before touching them. It is common to have special bookstands to hold the text, and the most beautiful of these rank among the masterpieces of Islamic art. The Qur'an itself has been both an object and source of artistic expression. Ornate copies of the Qur'an provide outstanding examples of the art of bookmaking. Furthermore, calligraphy—which commonly uses as its subject words or phrases from the Qur'an—has emerged as one of the most highly developed art forms in the Islamic world. Qur'anic calligraphy is used to decorate a wide range of objects, from buildings to ceramic and metal vessels, and even items of clothing.

The captivating sound of Qur'anic recitation is used to open most religious and official functions in the Islamic world, and skilled Qur'anic reciters enjoy a high status in the society. Given the importance accorded to the Qur'an, it should come as no surprise that the human conduit of the text, the Prophet Muhammad, is similarly venerated. The Qur'an refers to Muhammad as a blessing from God, a messenger, a warner, a guide, the bringer of good news, and good news in and of himself. Muslims commonly believe that Muhammad was a human being like any other who was chosen by God to be the last of his prophets and to be the instrument he used to reveal the Qur'an. The Qur'an itself emphasizes the ordinariness of Muhammad, commanding him to say that he was a mortal man like everyone else and chastising him for losing confidence and feeling insecure.

Nonetheless, it stands to reason that Muhammad would have been of outstanding moral character to begin with if an omniscient and omnipotent God was planning to use him as a prophet. Furthermore, once Muhammad took on the role of God's messenger and exemplar to humanity, God would hardly let him engage in any activity that would contradict the divine message. According to this viewpoint, then, Muhammad had to be free from sin (and possibly even from the capacity to sin), and any frailties or errors he displayed were themselves consciously added to his character by God to fulfill a divine purpose. Muhammad has therefore become the model of behavior for most Muslims who try and follow his example, or *Sunna*, and collected anecdotes of his life, called hadiths, represent a religious source second only to the Qur'an.

Muslim Meaning

Sunna is the custom or tradition of the Prophet Muhammad, which is used as a source of law and as an informal model of behavior in everyday life.

Understanding Hadith and Sunna

The word *hadith* primarily means a communication or a narrative in general. In Islamic terms, it has the particular meaning of a record of actions or sayings of the Prophet and his companions. In the latter sense, the whole body of the sacred tradition of Islam is called the "Hadith" and the formal study of it the "Science of Hadith."

Pre-Islamic Arabs considered it a virtue to follow the example of one's forefathers. But in the Islamic period, a person could hardly follow the example of ancestors who were not Muslim, so a new tradition, or Sunna, had to be found. This was the Sunna of Muhammad.

After Muhammad's death, the learned began to systematically develop the doctrine of duties and beliefs in accordance with the new conditions. After the early conquests, Islam covered an enormous area, and new ideas as well as institutions were borrowed from the conquered peoples. Nevertheless, in Islam only the Sunna of the Prophet and the original Muslim community could supply rules of conduct for the believers. This soon led to the deliberate forgery of traditions: Transmitters brought the words and actions of the Prophet into agreement with their own views and ideals.

Bet You Didn't Know

A very large portion of these "traditional" sayings ascribed to Muhammad deal with legal provisions, religious obligations, issues of what is permissible and what is forbidden, ritual purity, as well as with matters of etiquette and courtesy.

As early as the eighth century, certain Islamic scholars became extremely concerned about the large number of forged hadiths that were floating about and devised an elaborate system whereby some idea of the accuracy of a hadith could be established. According to the Muslim view, a hadith account can only be considered believable if its chain of transmission (or *isnad*) offers an unbroken series of reliable authorities.

The critical investigation of isnads has caused Muslim scholars to do research to ascertain the names and circumstances of the transmitters in a hadith account in order to investigate when and where they lived and which of them had been personally acquainted with one another. Scholars divide the Hadith into three main categories according to their reliability:

- *Sahih* (sound), or those hadiths that have flawless chains of transmission and reinforce something that is widely accepted in the Islamic community.

- *Hasan* (beautiful), which are considered reliable but whose authenticity is not totally beyond doubt.

- *Da'if* (weak), which are suspect in terms of either their content or the chain of transmitters.

The earliest collections of the Hadith, of which the best known was compiled by the respected scholar, Ibn Hanbal (d. 855), were arranged not according to their content but according to their transmitters (isnads). Later works were arranged by topic, two of which, those of al-Muslim (d. 875) and al-Bukhari (d. 870), are seen as so reliable that many Sunnis rank them just below the Qur'an itself as sacred texts.

> **On the Right Path**
>
> What is contained in the Hadith is the Sunna, or tradition, of Muhammad, consisting of his actions and sayings and those things to which he gave unspoken approval. Sunna has come to mean the practice of the greater Muslim community, and in this capacity it is often referred to as the "living Sunna." In theory the concepts of Sunna and Hadith are separate, but in practice they often coincide.

Muhammad had settled many questions posed to him not by revelation but by decisions made on a case-by-case basis, and the words and actions of the Prophet were recognized—even in his own lifetime—as worthy of imitation. It is for this reason that the Sunna of the Prophet was fixed in writing and became a standard of behavior alongside the Qur'an.

Religious scholars tried to answer questions concerning the relation between the two of them. In the earliest Islamic community, the Sunna appears to have been equal to the Qur'an in its authority. However, with the passage of time and conversion of non-Arab peoples to Islam, the Qur'an gained a centrality as scripture that outstripped the importance given to the Sunna, particularly in its written form of the Hadith.

In actual practice, many Muslims do not make a clear distinction between hadiths compiled by al-Bukhari or al-Muslim, and those that have been deemed fake by scholars. The result is an overall body of wisdom literature by which Muslims emphasize their high regard for Muhammad and learn lessons concerning ethics and morality that can then be applied to their everyday lives.

Veneration of Muhammad

Although at the level of religious doctrine and in the informal opinion of many Muslims the Qur'an occupies a higher and more central position in Islam than Muhammad does, the opposite often appears to be the case, particularly at the level of popular devotion. Most Muslims regard everything about Muhammad with deep veneration. He is widely regarded as the ideal human being and is therefore the model for imitation. Emulation of Muhammad ranges from seeing him as a model in legal and ethical matters to seemingly trivial details in everyday life, such as how to brush your teeth, wear your hair, or what food to eat.

Intercession or No?

A frequently mentioned characteristic of Islam as a religion is the value placed upon the direct link between individual human beings and God. The so-called orthodox tradition of the legal scholars and theologians does not recognize the existence of a clergy in Islam, nor of any form of sainthood in which living or dead people can intercede for other human beings.

Yet, many Muslims firmly believe in the possibility of intercession (a go-between), not just by Muhammad, but also by a variety of other saintly figures, including members of Muhammad's family, prominent mystical figures, or Sufis, and other individuals with whom miracles are associated or who are known to be uncommonly pious. The possibility of intercession is brought up in one of the most famous verses of the Qur'an: "Who is it that can intercede before Him except as He permits?" (2:255).

The issue of intercession is a major one throughout Islam, and involves questions not just of theology and the interpretation of scripture but also issues of class, culture, gender, and level of education. The acknowledgment of the possibility of intercession before God allows for the existence of saints and a clergy, and for a wide variety of religious expression. It is one of the major fault-lines along which one can divide the varieties of Muslim religious experience.

The Least You Need to Know

- God is referred to by his Arabic name Allah, most likely derived from *al-ilah*, literally meaning "The God."

- Muslims see their relationship with God as an intimate one in which God's creation of human beings is a blessing, and his laws and restrictions are an act of grace providing guidance in this life.

- For many Muslims the Qur'an is the single greatest sign of God in the physical universe; it provides instructions on how to live your life, and it acts as a source of ethical guidance.

- The word "hadith" primarily means a communication or a narrative in general; the whole body of the sacred tradition of Islam is called the "Hadith" and the formal study of it the "Science of Hadith."

- Muhammad is the model of behavior for most Muslims who try and follow his example, or Sunna, and collected anecdotes of his life, called hadiths, represent a religious source that are second only to the Qur'an.

- The "orthodox" tradition of the legal scholars and theologians does not recognize the existence of a clergy in Islam, yet many Muslims firmly believe in the possibility of a mediator between individuals and Allah.

Chapter 2

The Birth of Islam

In This Chapter

- Arabia and its religions
- Muhammad enters the world
- From Mecca to Medina

Islam's historical origins lie in the life of a man named Muhammad, who was born in the city of Mecca in present-day Saudi Arabia in around 570 C.E. and died in a nearby city called Medina in 632 C.E. In Muhammad's time, Arabia was culturally, politically, and economically impoverished relative to the large and wealthy empires that surrounded it.

To the north were the Byzantine Greek and Sassanian Persian Empires and to the south the affluent world of Abyssinia. Arabia itself was divided between the main Arabian plateau and a region called South Arabia (present-day Yemen), which had once been the seat of a thriving agricultural society but had fallen on poorer times.

Muhammad's Arabia

The plateau, where Muhammad was from, was an arid place in which the majority of people lived as nomads, accompanying their herds of camels, sheep, and goats from one place to another in search of good pasture. The few cities were located on oases, which provided the only reliable source of water for agriculture, and some were centers for trade among the people of Arabia and with the surrounding lands.

The Arabs of Muhammad's time lived in tribes that were large social groups held together by a shared ancestry, each being composed of a number of clans made up of several extended families. A family elder would be recognized as the leader of the clan, and the clan leaders together constituted the ruling council of a tribe. Tribal councils tried to operate through negotiation and consensus building, although powerful clans no doubt had much greater influence over tribal affairs than did weaker ones.

The Arabian peninsula had no central government or state, but existed in a state of balance between tribes on the one hand, and the mercantile and agrarian cities on the other. Nomads who belonged to the same or allied tribes as town-dwellers would often agree not to attack these places (or the caravans going to or from them).

Bet You Didn't Know

The majority of tribes in Arabia were patriarchal; however, there appear to have been some tribes in which lineage was passed down through the mother, and even in very patriarchal tribes it was not uncommon for women to hold property. A good example of this was Muhammad's first wife, Khadija, who was a wealthy widow, actively engaged in trade.

Arabia was located at the crossroads of many trade routes; goods brought by ship to Arabian ports were loaded onto camel caravans to be transported across the desert to distant markets. Mercantile cities were heavily dependent upon the east-west trade between the Indian Ocean and the Mediterranean, and on the north-south trade between Africa and the Byzantine and Sassanian Empires. Many nomadic tribes supported themselves by raiding caravans, so much so that the practice was considered an acceptable way of life and was covered by a code of conduct.

Arabia's Religions

Very little is known about the religious situation in Arabia at the time of Muhammad's birth. The surrounding empires had large Christian populations,

Abyssinia and the Byzantine Empire both being Christian kingdoms. Sassanian Persia (modern Iran) was officially *Zoroastrian*, a major religion of that time that survives today in very small numbers. Even so, Persia had a large Christian population. In addition, all the empires had significant Jewish populations.

Muslim Meaning

Zoroastrianism is a religion founded in Persia in the sixth century B.C.E. by the prophet Zoroaster; its sacred book is the Avesta. The religion is characterized by worshiping Ahura Mazda (their supreme god) who is in a cosmic struggle against Ahriman (the evil spirit).

There were clearly some Christians within Arabia, but their numbers appear to have been quite small and they were individual believers, not entire clans or tribes who regarded themselves as Christian. There was also no church based within Arabia. The number of Arabian Jews appears to have been much larger; there were entirely Jewish tribes, some of which seem to have moved to Arabia from Palestine after the destruction of the temple in Jerusalem by the Romans at the end of the first century C.E. There were probably many who, though not formally Jews, identified themselves as

Israelites and were familiar with the stories of the Hebrew prophets.

The majority of Arabs did not belong to any formal religion but believed in a combination of supernatural forces, some of which they identified as spirits and others as gods. The spirits were believed to inhabit natural objects such as rocks and trees and to have influence over human lives, whereas the gods were often identified with natural phenomena such as the sun, moon, and rain. Many Arabs viewed the god of the moon and traveling, named Allah (literally, "The God"), as the ancestor and leader of the others.

The pre-Islamic Arabs did not have a detailed moral and ethical code of the kind that was developed in Islamic, Christian, and Jewish theology, nor did they commonly believe in life after death. Instead, they were governed by rules of honor, courage, and hospitality. In the absence of a belief in the afterlife, the primary way to attain immortality was to live heroic lives full of extravagant acts of valor and generosity, which were then rendered into verse by tribal poets. The Arabs were in awe of the power of poetry and poets, and viewed them as supernaturally possessed figures to be both feared and revered, not only as artists but also as tribal historians.

In addition to poets, two other figures carried great respect in pre-Islamic Arab society. The first was the seer, who would foretell the future and attempt to solve problems as diverse as those of curing infertility and finding lost animals. The other was the judge, whose job it was to intercede in conflicts within a tribe and, more importantly, between tribes, as a way of avoiding violence.

> ![icon] **Bet You Didn't Know**
>
> Poets, seers, and judges hold relevance for early Islamic history because, during his career as a prophet, Muhammad displayed qualities of all three, enabling his critics to label him as a poet or seer in order to dismiss his religious claims.

Muhammad's Birth and Early Life

Muhammad's family belonged to the clan of Hashim in the tribe of Quraysh, an important merchant tribe with considerable influence in Mecca and the surrounding area. The Hashim clan, though not the most powerful in the tribe, was considered respectable. Mecca was home to a major shrine, called the *Ka'ba*, which was one of the few religious sites revered by people from all over Arabia. In their status as custodians of this site, the Quraysh tribe not only gained financially from the pilgrimage business but also in reputation, because of their exclusive control of the associated rituals. Several of these were later incorporated into the *Hajj* pilgrimage (see Chapter 7), which became a central rite in Islam.

Muslim Meaning

Hajj is a pilgrimage to the Ka'ba in Mecca, which constitutes one of the ritual obligations of Islam. The **Ka'ba** is a cubic building located in Mecca, believed to have been built by Abraham at God's command. It is the direction in which Muslims pray, in addition to being the focus of the Hajj.

Muhammad's father, Abdallah, died shortly before he was born, and his paternal guardianship was taken over by his grandfather, Abd al-Muttalib. When he was born, his mother, Amina, named him Ahmad while his grandfather named him Muhammad. The latter name became more common, although even to this day he is sometimes referred to as Ahmad.

Very little is known about Muhammad's childhood or about the period of his life before his career as a prophet began. The few things that we can consider to be factually true have been embellished by pious biographers who inserted real or imagined events into his early life in order to show that Muhammad was marked for greatness from the time of his birth.

As a very young child, Muhammad was sent to the desert to live with a nomadic tribe, a Meccan custom that perhaps derived from the desire to get children out of the unhygienic environment of the city, as well as from the belief that the nomads led a culturally "purer" Arab life. Muhammad lived with a foster family as a shepherd, and he retained a great deal of affection for them in later life, particularly for his foster mother, Halima.

According to a popular legend, one day while Muhammad was herding sheep he was visited by two angels who laid him down and opened up his chest. They then took out his heart and washed it in a golden basin filled with snow before replacing it and closing him up, which probably symbolizes the removal of all existing sin from his body. However, neither the notion of primordial sin nor the belief that one can inherit his or her parents' sins is prevalent in Islam.

Following this visitation, Muhammad's foster family began to fear for his safety and decided to return him to his mother before something bad happened to him. Shortly after his return to Mecca, both Muhammad's mother and grandfather died, and his guardianship was assumed by his paternal uncle, Abu Talib, a merchant who frequently traveled throughout Arabia. Muhammad accompanied his uncle on these expeditions, probably including one journey to Syria, and, in the process, not only learned the merchant's trade but also came in contact with a wider variety of people.

Muhammad's Youth

Upon reaching adulthood, Muhammad became a merchant himself and quickly gained a reputation for honesty and trustworthiness. A wealthy widow named Khadija noticed him and extended to Muhammad a marriage proposal, which he accepted. At the time of their wedding, Muhammad was 25 years old and Khadija was 40. In later life, Muhammad spoke fondly of the years he had spent with Khadija, who was the mother of the only children Muhammad had who survived past infancy.

In his adult years, Muhammad had developed the habit of retiring to a cave outside Mecca to meditate in private. On one such occasion he fell asleep, only to be awakened by an angelic being who commanded him: "Recite!" Muhammad replied by asking what he should recite, at which the angel only repeated his initial command. After the third time, the angel commanded this:

> Recite! In the name of your Lord Who created.
> Created man from a clot!
> Recite! And your Lord is Most Bountiful—
> He taught by the pen—
> Taught man that which he knew not! (Qur'an, 96:1–5)

This event occurred when Muhammad was 40 years old, and for the remainder of his life he continued to receive revelations, sometimes through the efforts of that angelic being whom he was to identify as Gabriel, and at others directly from God.

Initially Muhammad sought comfort from his wife Khadija, but over time, she convinced him to listen to the angel. Muhammad was convinced that he had been chosen as a prophet of God to bring a divine message to humankind about the existence of a unique, all-powerful God, a warning of an impending doomsday and judgment, and an encouragement to live a virtuous life.

Time to Leave Mecca ...

At first Muhammad's preaching was met with tolerance and curiosity, but as he started to gain converts, the leaders of Mecca began to perceive him as a threat and to persecute his followers. The majority of Muhammad's early followers were women, slaves, and the very poor, all of whom were extremely vulnerable to their powerful oppressors.

Fearing for their safety in Mecca, Muhammad and his followers began to search for a new place to live. It so happened that a nearby town, Yathrib, needed an impartial judge to arbitrate between two powerful tribes, and they extended Muhammad an invitation to move to Yathrib and deliver judgments. Muhammad agreed to do so only if certain conditions were fulfilled:

- That his family and followers be allowed to move with him

- That they would be supported until they could find means of livelihood for themselves
- That they were to be considered full citizens of the city, so that if the Meccans and their allies chose to attack the Muslims, all the citizens of Yathrib would fight on the side of the Muslims

The delegation from Yathrib agreed to these terms and a secret migration of Muslims from Mecca to this city began. Finally, when all but two of Muhammad's followers (his friend Abu Bakr and his cousin Ali) had reached Yathrib, he decided to move there himself. By this time, some of his opponents had realized that he represented a grave threat to their interests and had formed a pact to kill him. Hearing of their plan, Muhammad secretly left Mecca in the company of his closest friend and advisor, Abu Bakr, leaving Ali in his house.

Bet You Didn't Know

Ali was the son of Muhammad's uncle Abu Talib. He had come to live with Muhammad as his adopted son, married his daughter Fatima, and became one of the most important and influential people in the formative period of Islam.

That night, Muhammad's enemies surrounded his house. Ali served as a decoy by sleeping in

Muhammad's bed. When the Meccans finally broke into Muhammad's house and found Ali, they realized that Muhammad had slipped away and sent a search party to hunt him down. Legend has it that Muhammad and Abu Bakr hid in a cave to escape their pursuers, and that a spider wove a web covering the entrance to the cave. Seeing the spider web, the Meccans thought that no one had been inside in a while and turned away. After the search party had returned empty-handed, Muhammad and Abu Bakr made their way to Yathrib, and Ali followed as soon as he had settled all of Muhammad's financial and social obligations in Mecca.

The Great Emigration: The Hijra

The emigration of Muhammad and the Muslims from Mecca to Yathrib, which occurred in 622, marks the most important date in Islamic history. It is called the *Hijra*, or "Great Emigration"; the Muslims who emigrated are referred to as *Muhajirs* and those who helped them as *Ansar*. Great honor has been attached to both groups throughout Islamic history.

The Hijra signals the beginning of Islam as a social religion. In Mecca, Muhammad was mostly a "warner" and prophet bringing a message of monotheism (belief in one God) and urging people to repent of their immoral ways. In Yathrib, the religion began to evolve into a social phenomenon and developed a history and complex set of laws. The city was even renamed Madinat al-nabi ("City of the Prophet"), Medina for short.

Bet You Didn't Know

Any event in which a number of Muslims have had to flee from persecution to a safe haven is seen as a repetition of the Hijra. The Hijra also marks the start of the Islamic calendar, which is used for all religious events and is the official calendar in many countries to this day.

While at Medina, the revelations that Muhammad received began to emphasize social laws and a sense of history, which showed Muhammad and his religion to be a continuation of the sacred tradition of the Hebrew prophets. Muhammad rapidly rose from the status of a simple prophet to that of the social, religious, and political leader of an entire community. As such, he resembled religious figures such as Moses, David, and Solomon much more than he did Jesus or the Buddha.

The Meccans perceived the Muslim community of Medina as a growing threat and engaged in three battles with them, each of which resulted in Muhammad's cause becoming much stronger. Finally in 630 C.E., the city of Mecca surrendered to Muhammad and he entered it, guaranteeing the life and property of its citizens. The only major events were the executions of a few poets who had ridiculed Muhammad and his religion, and the removal of all pagan religious objects from the Ka'ba.

Muhammad performed a pilgrimage to the Ka'ba and then returned to Medina, which he now considered his home. He made one more journey to Mecca before his death; referred to as the "Farewell Pilgrimage," it still serves as the model for one of the most important Islamic rituals, the Hajj (see Chapter 7).

Shortly after his return from the Farewell Pilgrimage, Muhammad fell gravely ill and confined himself to the house of his wife A'isha whom he had married in Mecca several years after Khadija's death. He died in her bed around midday on June 8, 632 C.E. According to a tradition stating that prophets should be buried where they die, Muhammad was buried in A'isha's chamber. Later on, it was converted into a shrine and serves as an important pilgrimage site to this day.

Bet You Didn't Know

A'isha—Muhammad's wife and Abu Bakr's daughter—outlived Muhammad by several decades and is one of the most important sources of doctrinal and historical information in the formative period of Islam.

The Least You Need to Know

- The pre-Islamic Arabs did not have a detailed moral and ethical code of the kind that was developed in Islamic, Christian, and Jewish theology; instead, they were governed by rules of honor, courage, and hospitality.

- The angel Gabriel gave Muhammad (at the age of 40) a divine message to humankind about the existence of a unique, all-powerful God, a warning of an impending doomsday and judgment, and an encouragement to live a virtuous life.

- Some of the most important and influential people in the formative period of Islam were as follows: Ali, the son of Muhammad's uncle Abu Talib, who came to live with Muhammad as his adopted son and married Muhammad's daughter Fatima; Khadija, Muhammad's first wife who is remembered as the first convert to Islam; A'isha, a later wife of Muhammad and daughter of his closest friend and advisor Abu Bakr.

- The Great Emigration, or Hijra, of Muhammad and the Muslims from Mecca to Yathrib (Medina), which occurred in 622, marks the beginning of the Islamic lunar calendar.

The Islamic Community After Muhammad

In This Chapter

- Succession struggles following Muhammad's death
- The Sunnis and the Shi'is
- Three main branches of Shi'is
- Sunni theology and law as the "orthodox" Islamic tradition

Muhammad died without appointing a definite successor. Although it was very clear that there would be no prophets after him, no one was sure what the role of the next leader should be. The elders of the Islamic community decided that Muhammad's closest male companion, Abu Bakr, who was also one of the earliest converts to Islam, should lead the community after his death.

Abu Bakr died only two years after Muhammad and was succeeded by another respected companion of Muhammad named Umar. It was during

Umar's 10-year leadership and the 12 years of his successor, Uthman, that the Islamic community spread out of Arabia and expanded from the Mediterranean shores of North Africa to the Central Asian steppes. It was also during their time that the revelations received by Muhammad were organized into the Qur'an.

Post-Muhammad Leaders

The leaders of the Islamic community after Muhammad were neither prophets nor kings. Instead, they were known as Caliphs (*khalifa* in Arabic), a word that means "representative" or "delegate," implying that they did not rule on their own authority but only as the representatives of God and his Prophet.

After Uthman's death there was some confusion as to who should be the next Caliph. Many people felt that the honor should go to Muhammad's cousin and son-in-law, Ali. Others, however, favored Uthman's cousin Mu'awiya. Encouraged by their respective supporters, both men were declared Caliph and a civil war ensued. In the course of the dispute, Ali was murdered by an assassin and *Muawiya* successfully seized power for himself and his family, laying the foundations of the first Islamic dynasty, known as the Umayyads (a reference to *Mu'awiya's* tribe).

Even though the Umayyads were in almost complete control, the dispute between the supporters of Ali and the Umayyads did not end. It took an even more serious turn when Ali's son Husayn and many of his family members were massacred by troops loyal to Mu'awiya's son, Yazid, in 680 C.E.

On the Right Path

The majority of pious Muslims today believe that with the rise of the Umayyad dynasty, the pristine institution of the Caliphate came to an end; they consider the first four Caliphs as truly virtuous, as a result of which those four are referred to as "Rightly-Guided." Even so, it was under the 100-year rule of the Umayyads that most of the lands still identified with Islam were conquered, and the Islamic empire extended from Spain to Pakistan.

Disillusioned by the political conflict, many Muslims withdrew into a quiet contemplation of their faith. Others devoted themselves to preaching among the citizens of the newly conquered lands, while still others dedicated their lives to the study of the Qur'an and the traditions of Muhammad and his companions. It was primarily through the efforts of such people that the Islamic world developed a rich and vibrant tradition of theology and philosophy and that the citizens of very diverse lands converted to the new religion.

And So the Schism Begins

The succession struggles following Muhammad's death served as the primary catalysts for the initial sectarian schism within Islam, one that persists to this day. One faction maintained that Ali should have been the rightful leader of the Islamic community, and is known as the *Shi'at Ali* ("Faction of Ali") or *Shi'is* for short (this is the same word as Shi'ah and Shi'ite). The Shi'i position sees the first three Caliphs as usurpers, who deprived Ali of his birthright.

. Muslim Meaning

Shi'i is the name given to a number of Muslim sects, all of which separated from the Sunni Muslim majority over the status of Ali as the successor to Muhammad. Ali is Muhammad's cousin and son-in-law, considered to be the first Imam by Shi'i Muslims and the fourth Caliph by Sunnis. He is one of the most important figures in early Islam.

This belief is supported by many hadiths according to which, in his absence, Muhammad used to designate Ali as the temporary leader of the Islamic community. The most famous of these is known as the Hadith of Ghadir Khum, named after an oasis between Mecca and Medina. According to this tradition, on his return from his final visit to Mecca,

Muhammad clasped Ali's hand in his and declared before the assembled crowd: "For whomever I have been a protector (mawla), Ali is his protector."

The implications of this hadith ride on the multiple meanings of the word *mawla*. Scholars of the Sunni sect—many of whom consider this hadith reliable since it appears in the compendium of the great Sunni scholar Ibn Hanbal with no less than 10 variant readings—have taken it to mean protector or leader in a very narrow sense, implying that Ali was to be an authority only in very specific contexts.

The Shi'is Say ...

The Shi'is see it as a public declaration by Muhammad that community leadership should remain forever in the hands of the *ahl al-bayt* ("members of the household"). Few other hadiths support the Shi'i assertion, although they claim this is because the record was falsified by the supporters of Abu Bakr and later by the Umayyads. The Shi'is have their own collections of hadiths that contradict the Sunni view of events, the most important being the *Nahj al-balagha*, which is comprised of sayings and sermons attributed to Ali.

Several accounts within the work provide insight into the Shi'i position regarding leadership after Muhammad:

> The family members of the Prophet (on him be blessings and peace) are the locus of divine

mystery; they are where his commandments are guarded and the repositories of his knowledge, refuges for his wisdom, sanctuaries for his books, and mountain strongholds for his religion. Through them did he straighten the bowing of [the religion's] back, and through them did he banish the trembling of its flesh.

A particularly eloquent reading of the events that led to the political marginalization of Ali and the Prophet's household is found in Ali's *al-Khutba al-shaqshaqiya* or "Braying Sermon." It is so named because Ali was interrupted while speaking and refused to continue it, stating that the sermon had been extemporaneous like the braying of a camel, which starts spontaneously and stops in the same way.

According to this account, while the family of the Prophet had been busy with his burial, Abu Bakr had usurped power for himself without consulting Ali or any of Muhammad's other close relatives. On his death, Abu Bakr had nominated his ally Umar to be the leader of the Islamic community even though this form of successorship was in complete violation of Muhammad's wishes. On Umar's death, a council was convened to name a successor; it included Ali but was unfairly packed with supporters of Uthman. This ushered in a particularly dark period of oppression and nepotism that the virtuous members of the Islamic community could do little more than bear in silence.

Ali's silence in the face of these unjust transfers of power is explained by his desire to prevent bloodshed and division within the young Islamic community. However, when Uthman passed leadership to his reckless cousin Mu'awiya, Ali was forced to intervene at the request of virtuous members of the community, who repeatedly pleaded with him to deliver them from Mu'awiya's tyrannical rule.

The Sunnis Say ...

Sunni historians and theologians interpret the events such that Abu Bakr was reluctant to assume leadership and only did so for the express purpose of holding the Islamic community together as it weathered the crisis presented by the death of its prophet. They believed it was evident that he was the best person to assume this role because of his seniority in age and closeness to Muhammad. His selection of Umar as his successor was founded on a similar closeness to the Prophet and seniority as a convert.

The Sunnis do not deny Ali's seniority as an early convert or his reputation for religious knowledge or zeal in service to Islam. They do, however, traditionally maintain that Ali was too young at the time of Muhammad's and Abu Bakr's deaths to become the leader of the community. In so doing, they consciously deny the kinship-based claim to leadership (which is so central to the Shi'i view), seeing it as antithetical to Islamic teachings. The strength of the Sunni position lies in the claim that it was preferable to accept a less-than-ideal leader than to risk the destruction of the Muslim community through civil war.

> **Bet You Didn't Know** _____
>
> The name of the Sunni sect derives from the word *Sunna* (tradition) and is actually an abbreviation for a much longer term meaning "The People of Tradition (*Sunna*) and the Community," which implies a commitment to political quietism and a desire to avoid splitting into factions at whatever cost.

Sunnis vs. Shi'is

At most times in history, the Sunni sect has taken a very inclusive attitude and tried to count as many Muslims as it could within the Sunni umbrella, even when it meant that the notion of acceptable Sunni belief had to be expanded. At the same time, being a Sunni does not necessarily imply that one agrees with the way the Sunni Islamic world is being governed, simply that one believes that it is more important to keep the Muslim community safe than it is to fight a bad ruler.

Sunnis do, however, harbor some antipathy toward the Shi'is for the disrespect they show toward figures who are highly venerated in Sunni circles. Indeed, members of some Shi'i sects continue to ritualistically curse Abu Bakr, Umar, Uthman, and A'isha, and a holiday known as *Umar-kushi* ("Umar killing") was commemorated in southwestern Iran until the middle of the twentieth century to celebrate the death of Umar.

However, such practices have relied on communal segregation for their survival, and as Shi'i and Sunni societies are drawn closer together through developing global infrastructures and shared national interests, conciliatory leaders on both sides try their best to minimize their differences in belief and practice.

In recent times, Shi'ism has developed a negative reputation for a perceived propensity toward violence, as evidenced by events in Iran following the Islamic Revolution of 1979, and in southern Lebanon where a Shi'i militia has waged a lengthy guerrilla war against Israel and rival militias within Lebanon. In actual fact, much of Shi'i history has been one of political withdrawal and an outright rejection of worldly power.

After the assassination of Ali in 661 and the martyrdom of his son Husayn in 680, the Shi'is were not to wield political power for quite some time, as a result of which they spent less time emphasizing the political dimension of Shi'ism and more on developing elaborate theological ideas. However, the early political experiences had a direct bearing on Shi'i beliefs, which emphasize the importance of martyrdom and persecution.

Sectarian Division Within the Shi'is

There are three main branches of Shi'ism:

- Zaydis
- Twelvers
- Isma'ilis

All are united by a common belief that the only legitimate leader of the Muslim community is a descendant of Ali and his wife Fatima, the daughter of the Prophet. This leader is known as the *Imam*, and is considered superior to other human beings on account of his bloodline. The three main Shi'i sects agree on the identities of the first four Imams. There is disagreement over the fifth, with the majority believing that Husayn's grandson, Muhammad al-Baqir (d. 731), was the rightful Imam, and a minority following al-Baqir's brother, Zayd (d. 740), on account of which they are called Zaydis.

Muslim Meaning

Imam literally means "leader." It is a term used for anyone who leads prayers in a mosque. More important, it is the title of the rightful leader of the Muslim community in the Shi'i sect.

Zaydis

Zayd was the first person after the massacre of Husayn and his family to try to wrest political power from the Umayyads by force. After spending a year in preparation in the heavily Shi'i city of Kufa in Iraq, he came out with a group of followers but was killed in battle.

Zaydi beliefs are similar to those of the major Shi'i sect, that of the Twelvers. The major difference is that Zaydis believe that any descendant of Ali and Fatima can be the Imam, regardless of whether they are descended from Husayn or his elder brother Hasan. In order to be acknowledged as the Imam, a person must have the ability to resort to the sword if necessary. For this reason, unlike in Twelver Shi'ism, no person who remains hidden can be considered the rightful Imam.

The Zaydi Imam is also required to possess high moral character and religious learning. If a person does not live up to all these requirements, he cannot be recognized as a full Imam but is an inferior Imam of either martial skill or learning only. Leaders whose political and intellectual strength is only enough to keep the Zaydi religious claim alive are called Da'is, a term shared by the third Shi'i sect, the Isma'ilis. The high standards required of a Zaydi Imam, combined with the concept of the Da'i, allows for the possibility that there might be an age without an Imam, when the community is led by Da'is.

Bet You Didn't Know

Zaydi Shi'ism never gained a great following, and in modern times is almost entirely limited to the country of Yemen.

Twelvers

Those members of the Shi'i community who did not accept Zayd as the rightful Imam remained in agreement for two more generations. The sixth Imam of this group, Ja'far al-Sadiq (d. 765), is especially important because he was a very great scholar who is also highly regarded by the Sunnis. The major Shi'i school of religious law is called "Ja'fari" because of him.

After the death of Ja'far al-Sadiq, this Shi'i group divided into two, the first being Isma'ilis, who recognized his elder son Isma'il (d. 765) as the rightful leader; the second followed his younger son, Musa (d. 799). This latter sect continued following a chain of Imams until the twelfth in succession from Ali, Muhammad al-Mahdi, who vanished in 874 C.E. His followers, thereafter known as Twelver Shi'is, believed that he had gone into a form of supernatural hiding and would return as the messiah at the end of the world.

Twelver Shi'is have a complex theory concerning the nature of the Imam, which derives in large part from writings attributed to Ja'far al-Sadiq. In every age there is an Imam who represents God on Earth, and who designates his successor by giving him a body of knowledge covering the inner and outer meanings of the Qur'an. The institution of the Imam is a covenant between God and human beings, and all believing Twelver Shi'is are required to acknowledge and follow the Imam of their age. Twelver Shi'is regard Imams as free of sin; they serve as the doorway to God and convey his message directly.

After the disappearance of the twelfth imam, envoys (*wakils*) acting on his behalf claimed that they were in direct contact with him. When the fourth of them died in 939 C.E., no one else succeeded in his claim to be the wakil of the vanished Imam. The period from then on came to be known as the "Greater Occultation," as distinct from the earlier one, which was called the "Lesser Occultation."

During this later period, which extends until today, Twelver Shi'ism developed an elaborate clerical system that takes care of the religious needs of the Shi'i community. The highest rank of this clergy is believed to be inspired by the Imam and is given the right to engage in independent reasoning (*ijtihad*). In actual fact, since the sixteenth century, Shi'i clerics have been extremely conservative in their exercise of ijtihad and, for all practical purposes, act exactly the way a Sunni scholar does in the study of law.

> ### Muslim Meaning
>
> **Ijtihad** is the independent reasoning of a qualified Islamic legal scholar, referred to as a *mujtahid* or *faqih* (scholar who studies Islamic jurisprudence).

Isma'ilis

Some Shi'is maintained that it was Isma'il and not his younger brother Musa who was the rightful seventh Imam, despite the fact that Isma'il died before his father, Ja'far al-Sadiq. According to Isma'ili doctrine, before dying, Isma'il designated his son Muhammad ibn Isma'il as his successor, and the line of Imams continued with him.

A fundamental feature of early Isma'ili thought was the division of all knowledge into two levels, an outer, exoteric one (*zahir*) and an inner, esoteric one (*batin*). The exoteric level of knowledge changes with every prophet and every scripture. The esoteric level is concealed under the words of the scriptures and their laws, and conveys an immutable truth that can only be made apparent through a process of interpretation (called *ta'wil*). This is the exclusive prerogative of the Imam or of his deputies.

One of the most interesting aspects of Isma'ili thought is the concept of cyclical time. History goes through a cycle of seven eras, each inaugurated by a prophet who publicly announces his message using a scripture. The first six of these prophets are Adam, Noah, Abraham, Moses, Jesus, and Muhammad. These prophets are accompanied by a silent companion who is the guardian of the esoteric dimension of the scripture.

Muslim Meaning

Zahir and batin are terms used in Shi'i thought (and Sufism—see Chapter 5) for the hidden meanings of a text, particularly the Qur'an. Zahir is the outer, exoteric level and batin is the inner, esoteric level.

In the cycle of Muhammad, Muhammad ibn Isma'il is the seventh Imam and will return in the future to serve as the public prophet of his own (the seventh) prophetic cycle, bringing the entire cycle of seven to an end and our world with it. Until his return, Isma'ilis believe that the hidden batin (inner) knowledge should be kept secret, and revealed only to initiated believers.

The Isma'ilis became extremely powerful in North Africa in the tenth century and founded a dynasty known as the Fatimids, which for a brief period posed a threat to the absolute political authority of the Sunni Caliphs of the Abbasid dynasty. The great city of Cairo was founded by these Isma'ilis, as was Cairo's famous university, Al-Azhar. In later times, this university became one of the most important centers of Sunni learning and continues in that role to this day.

Over the centuries, Isma'ilism has split into a number of different sects, especially the rival followers of the two brothers, Nizar (d. 1095) and al-Musta'li (d. 1101). The Fatimid rulers supported the religious claims of al-Musta'li, forcing the followers of Nizar to flee Fatimid territories or else to hide for fear of persecution.

The Fatimid Empire was destroyed by the rise to power of the Sunni Ayyubid dynasty, but not before Isma'ili scholars patronized by the Fatimids had left a lasting impact on Islamic philosophy and mysticism. Nizar's followers found refuge in the Syrian and Iranian mountains, and dispersed after the Mongol invasion of the thirteenth century. In the nineteenth century, the Iranian monarch gave the well-known title Agha Khan to the Imam of one of their sub-sects, the Qasimshahis.

Today, Isma'ilis remain fragmented, with Nizaris concentrated in northern Pakistan as well as parts of Afghanistan, Tajikistan, and India. The line of al-Musta'li is concentrated around the Arabian Sea, on the western coast of India, and in Pakistan and Yemen.

The Umayyads and the Abbasids

From the time of the Umayyad Caliphs onward (661–750) virtually all Muslim areas, with the exception of Iran after the sixteenth century, have had a Sunni majority. Most of the areas that converted to Islam after its initial rapid expansion in the seventh and eighth centuries also adopted the Sunni version of the religion, as a result of which Sunni theology and law are widely regarded as representing the "orthodox" Islamic tradition.

The Umayyads proved to be great state builders as were the Abbasid Caliphs (750–1258) after them. The Abbasids, who on occasion tried to reconcile the Sunni-Shi'i schism, were also active champions of scholarship and the arts.

Their rule is also frequently referred to as the Classical Islamic Age, when the major points of religious doctrine, law, theology, and philosophy were addressed in ways that framed their discussion until modern times and, arguably, continue to shape the ideas and behavior of traditionalists. The next chapter will be a brief overview of some of the key developments in Islamic theology and law.

On the Right Path

The Abbasid dynasty heralded a period of unprecedented prosperity in the Islamic world, the mythic glory of which has been immortalized in works such as *The One Thousand and One Nights* (more commonly known in English as *The Arabian Nights*).

The Least You Need to Know

- The leaders of the Islamic community after Muhammad were known as Caliphs, a word that means "representative" or "delegate," implying that they did not rule on their own authority but only as the representatives of God and his Prophet.

- The Shi'i faction of Islam believe that Muhammad publicly declared that community leadership should remain forever in the hands of the *ahl al-bayt* ("members of the household").

- The Sunnis deny the kinship-based claim to leadership after Muhammad, seeing it as antithetical to Islamic teachings; the strength of the Sunni position lies in the claim that it was preferable to accept a less-than-ideal leader than to risk the destruction of the Muslim community through civil war.

- The three main Shi'i sects agree on the identities of the first four Imams; there is disagreement over the fifth and again over the seventh.

- The Umayyads were great state builders, as were the Abbasids after them. The Abbasids, who on occasion tried to reconcile the Sunni-Shi'i schism, were also active champions of scholarship and the arts.

Chapter 4

Islamic Theology and Laws

In This Chapter

- Questions behind the theology
- Rules and values as guiding principles
- Jurisprudence and the people

It is impossible to provide a comprehensive account of Islamic theology and law in such a brief space, but their central aspects, particularly those formulated in the Classical period, are easily outlined in this chapter.

Keep in mind that the intricate details of theological and legal debates have little direct bearing on the religious lives of most Muslims. Nonetheless, over a period of time theological ideas have some influence in society, just as societal practices affect the content and nature of scholarly debate. More importantly, members of society can be directly affected by developments in law inasmuch as they see Islamic law as a guiding principle in their lives and are subjected to it by the judicial and police powers of a state.

The Theology Behind It All

As a prophet, Muhammad's role was more that of a preacher than a theologian. However, the Qur'an brings up many philosophical and theological questions regarding the nature of God, such as the following:

- What is God's relationship to our world?
- What about the problem of evil?
- What is the place occupied by human beings in the divine plan for the universe?

On the Right Path

Kalam is distinct from Islamic philosophy, in that the philosophical tradition is derived very consciously and directly from the world of Greek (and, to a lesser extent, Persian) thought. This is evident even from the word used for philosophy, which is *Falsafa,* an Arabic adaptation of the Greek word *philosophia.*

As the Islamic world expanded to absorb new cultures, many new philosophical questions emerged. Some of these issues were already being discussed in the newly converted territories; others were brought up by the theological debates that occurred as Islam came into competition with Christianity and Zoroastrianism (refer to Chapter 2), which were the major religions of that region; still others emerged as a result of political and social crises that plagued the early Muslim community.

The term most commonly used for theology in the Islamic world is *Kalam*, which literally means "speech" or "dialectic." This gives a clear sense of the fact that Islamic theology emerged in an environment where theological issues were being publicly debated.

Many of the major questions that were discussed in the earliest Islamic theological circles arose out of the political crises that followed the assassinations of the Caliphs Umar, Uthman, and Ali, and from the civil wars that resulted in the division between the Sunni and Shi'i sects. The main questions dealt with who was the rightful leader of the community, and what was the status of a believer who committed a grave sin (since the killers of the early Caliphs were all Muslims).

As theological schools grew within the Islamic world, the questions being debated became more theoretical and abstract. The main issues concerned the relationship between God's omnipotence and human responsibility. This led to more abstract discussions of the nature of God and of how human beings gained the ability to differentiate between right and wrong and to commit good and bad actions.

After the murder of Uthman and the emergence of sectarian divisions in the Islamic world, four major schools of thought emerged, representing the spectrum of Islamic theological opinions.

Qadariya: If You Sin, You Don't Believe

The first major school of thought, the Qadariya, was the most actively opposed to the Umayyad dynasty. The Qadariya believed that human beings have such extensive power over their actions that they can determine the commission and outcome of their acts. It is from the belief in human ability or determination (*qudra*) that the Qadariya get their name.

Since human beings had complete freedom of action, and their deeds were a perfect mirror of their belief, anyone who committed a grave sin must be a disbeliever.

Jabriya: It Wasn't My Fault

The second major school of thought was called the Jabriya, who took a diametrically opposite view to the original Qadariya. They believed that divine compulsion (*jabr*) created human actions and that human beings had absolutely no freedom in committing good or bad actions. Since God was the direct source of all acts, a human being could not be held responsible for committing a grave sin and therefore would still be considered a Muslim.

Murji'a: It's Up to God

The Murji'a occupied a position in between the Qadariya and the Jabriya. They believed that it was not possible for human beings to pass judgment over the status of another human being's faith. Instead, based on a Qur'anic verse, they believed that a grave sinner's future was held in suspense awaiting God's decision.

Khawarij: Mirror, Mirror ...

The last major group was called the Khawarij. Like the Qadariya, they believed that actions were the perfect mirror of an individual's faith. Unlike them, however, they tended to be extremely politically active. They felt it was the duty of every true Muslim to depose, by force if necessary, any leader who had strayed from the correct path.

Bet You Didn't Know

The Khawarij had originally supported Ali in his competition with Mu'awiya, but when Ali agreed to human arbitration (as opposed to letting God make the decision on the battlefield), they deserted him and came to be very distinct from his supporters, the Shi'is.

Start of Theological Schools

By the end of the eighth century, the trends of the early schools of thought had developed to the point that full-fledged theological schools had emerged within the Islamic world. The most famous of these is called the Mu'tazila, which for 40 years in the mid-ninth century held sway as the official theological school of the Sunni world.

Many religious scholars were mistreated if their beliefs did not coincide with those of the Mu'tazila. But when the Mu'tazila lost their official patronage, they came to be seen as heretical and were themselves victims of discrimination and persecution. This period of "inquisition" did nonetheless produce one benefit—a greater formalization of Islamic thought. The Mu'tazila were largely replaced by the Ash'ariya school, named for a scholar called al-Ash'ari (d. 935), a disillusioned former Mu'tazila theologian.

The two schools took quite different stands on a range of issues. For instance, whereas the Mu'tazila saw God's attributes (for example, references in the Qur'an to his compassion and mercy, even his hands and throne) as distinct from his essence and therefore noneternal, the Ash'ariya believed that God does indeed have eternal attributes, such as knowledge, sight, and speech. To the Ash'ariya, such "humanlike" qualities are real—it is just that we humans cannot understand their true meaning. Similarly, the Ash'ariya regard the Qur'an as the eternal speech of God, while the Mu'tazila believe that it could be replaced by another revealed scripture, if God so willed.

Unlike the Mu'tazila, the Ash'ariya implicitly accepted the vision of God that is promised in the afterlife. They also believed that the omnipotent God had willed both good and evil in the world. At the same time, the Ash'ariya felt that humans were accountable for their actions. From this they deduced that sinners could remain Muslim, yet still could be punished in hell for their crimes.

These differences between the Mu'tazila and Ash'ariya hinged on their different understandings of the power of human reason.

- The Ash'ariya recognized that human beings have some degree of free will and power of reasoning, but felt that these human abilities are extremely limited when compared to the omniscience and omnipotence of God.

- The Mu'tazila had great faith in the powers of the human intellect and refused to accept that certain things lay beyond human understanding.

Both positions have basis in the Islamic philosophical tradition, from which Islamic theology derived many of its ideas.

Islamic Law: The Shari'a

Islamic religious law (Shari'a) is an elaborate and dynamic system that has been evolving from the time of Muhammad until the present. It continues to be taken very seriously by a large number of Muslims, who use its rules and values as guiding principles in their lives. They consider the law to be one of the most remarkable aspects of their religion.

Islamic Law Sources

Islamic law is believed to be the collected prescriptions dictated by God for the running of the universe. The Qur'an provides very clear rules on issues as diverse as how to perform acts of worship, what not to eat, and how to distribute inheritance property. However, it does not provide clear rules for all the innumerable situations encountered in the course of human life.

The Islamic community did not see this as a problem when they had the living example of the Prophet to follow. Nor did the generations immediately after the death of Muhammad, because his memory was very much alive in the community: People felt they had a good idea of what Muhammad would have done in any given situation. However, as generations passed and the Islamic community spread to new cultures and was faced with new situations, it was more and more difficult to use the practices of Muhammad to guide all aspects of life.

It therefore became necessary to develop a system of law that provided a method by which rules could be developed to deal with new situations. This system is called *Fiqh* and is considered to have four principles called *Usul al-fiqh* (Principles of Jurisprudence):

- The Qur'an
- Sunna
- Reasoning by analogy *(qiyas)*
- Consensus of the community *(ijma)*

Principles of Jurisprudence

The primary source of Islamic law is the Qur'an. Rules and precepts that are clearly stated in the Qur'an are not open to debate and must be accepted at face value. Thus, for example, since the Qur'an explicitly forbids the eating of pork, Shari'a-observing Muslims see no need to consult other authorities.

If the Qur'an does not provide clear rules on a question of law, then you look to the examples of the Prophet or his Sunna.

The concept of Sunna is open to interpretation, since the vast number of individual hadiths sometimes contradict one another; furthermore, the concept of "living tradition" can cause conflict because not everyone agrees on which traditions of a society are in keeping with what Muhammad would have done and which are innovations.

On the Right Path

Often translated as "tradition," Sunna is the way Muhammad lived his life (refer to the section "Understanding Hadith and Sunna" in Chapter 1). This is preserved as "living Sunna" in the anecdotes concerning Muhammad's actions, which are known as hadiths.

From the ninth century onward, Muslim jurists have struggled to balance the Qur'an and Sunna, and to derive laws from these sources that can then be applied to new situations. This normally involves reasoning by analogy (the third Principle of Jurisprudence) and consensus of the community (the fourth). This system of independent legal reasoning to come up with new laws is called ijtihad, and someone who is qualified to engage in it is called a mujtahid.

Sunni Muslim Jurists

Sunni Muslim jurists belong to four schools that differ as to whether or not they put more trust in the textual sources of Qur'an and Hadith, or in the human ability to reason by analogy. These schools are called ...

- Maliki
- Hanbali
- Hanafi
- Shafi'i

The Maliki school is traditionally strongest in North Africa, and considers the "living Sunna" of the community to be more reliable than human reason. The Hanbali school is strongest in Saudi Arabia; it has historically given a great deal of weight to the literal interpretation of written texts, so much so that some Hanbali scholars insisted that an unreliable hadith should be preferred over a strong example of reasoning by analogy.

The Shafi'i and Hanafi schools together account for the majority of Sunni Muslims and have a wide distribution, the Shafi'i school being more popular among the Arabs of the Middle East and in Indonesia, and the Hanafi school being more accepted in South and Central Asia and in Turkey.

Bet You Didn't Know

Since the sixteenth century, the Hanafi school has largely replaced the Shafi'i school as the most influential legal tradition in the Islamic world. The Hanafi and Shafi'i schools use the principle of ijtihad (independent reasoning) to a much greater degree than do the Hanbali and Maliki schools.

An Example Helps

The best way to explain how the Principles of Jurisprudence work is to use an example, such as whether or not it is permissible to use a loudspeaker to make the Islamic call to prayer. Of course, neither the Qur'an nor the Hadith has any explicit reference to loudspeakers (or any other electrical device). On the other hand, there are several places in the Qur'an where you are encouraged to pray.

There are also hadith accounts that state that the Prophet appointed a particular person named Bilal to make the call to prayer because of his strong and attractive voice, and that this man used to stand on high ground to make the call so that it would carry farther. Reasoning by analogy, a legal scholar would argue that the Qur'an encourages prayer as an activity, and that the Prophet appointed Bilal to make the call to prayer precisely so that his voice would reach out to the widest possible audience.

The fact that Bilal stood on high ground also indicates that the Prophet wanted the call to prayer to reach as far as possible. Since a loudspeaker in no way changes the call to prayer but only makes it louder, thereby allowing it to be heard by more people, it should be permitted by Islamic law. If there was little or no objection to this legal opinion and several other judges arrived at a similar decision, there would be a consensus of opinion over the use of loudspeakers in making the call to prayer and they would be accepted by Islamic law (as, in fact, they have been).

Get the Scholars Straight

In practice, by the fourteenth century, many parts of the Islamic world had developed specialized offices dealing with the practice of law. The scholar who engaged in the theoretical study and interpretation of Islamic law was called a *faqih*. People with questions concerning the law would go to someone called a *mufti*, who was normally appointed by the ruler for the specific purpose of answering questions concerning the Shari'a.

At other times, the mufti was a highly respected faqih who became a mufti simply because he gained a reputation among the local populace as a good, reliable scholar. The mufti's answer to questions is called a *fatwa*, best translated as a legal opinion or decree. In theory, the mufti's opinion is binding on the person who posed the legal question. In practice, people frequently ignore the mufti's opinion if it displeases them, largely because there is no institution that enforces his decision.

The office of a judge, that is, someone who presides over a court and has the power of the state and its police to enforce his opinions, is fulfilled by a *qadi*. Qadis are government officials and are appointed by the rulers. Many faqihs consider government employment to be inappropriate for a scholar of law because of the temptation to compromise in matters of principle.

Ritual vs. Interpersonal

The system of Islamic law, or Shari'a, attempts to regulate all aspects of human life. It divides activities into the ritual and devotional acts by which human beings communicate with God and the myriad details of relationships between human beings.

In an attempt to take a comprehensive position on all aspects of human life, legal scholars have created a scale upon which they judge every human activity, be it ritual or interpersonal. At one extreme lie those activities—most of which are ritual obligations—which all Shari'a-observing Muslims are required to do; at the other end of the scale are behaviors that are categorically forbidden, such as worshiping a deity other than Allah. Key points on the scale between these two extremes are occupied by actions that are recommended (for example, showing hospitality to strangers) and those that are discouraged (for example, being cruel to animals).

Although many Muslims are not consciously aware of the degree to which Islamic beliefs and practices vary from one cultural context to another, the Shari'a legal tradition is based upon liberal accommodation to the particularities of context. Scholars of the stature of al-Shafi'i (d. 820, after whom the Shafi'i school is named) and al-Shaybani (d. 805, possibly the most influential figure in the Hanafi school) insisted that jurists should never rely completely on legal precedent but should look at the details of each case that comes before them, because the circumstances of every individual are unique.

This attitude toward law has prevented Shari'a from developing as a codified legal system. Some modern Islamic countries have attempted to formalize the Shari'a in order to use it as a national legal code on the model of European ones, but they have met with limited success.

Bet You Didn't Know

There is considerable regional variation in what is understood to be permissible and forbidden under Shar'ia law, particularly in dietary matters. On occasion, these differences derive from the distinctive legal traditions of various schools, although the schools' attitudes toward the permissibility of edible items are often determined by the region's food habits or dietary history. Furthermore, it is doubtful whether the average Muslim resident of a particular locale makes the distinction between what is normal in his or her own region's legal tradition and what is normative for Islam as a whole. Thus, many Sunni Muslims from the west coast of India consider lobster, crabs, and mollusks forbidden (a belief shared by Twelver Shi'is); but Muslims from Turkey and Lebanon, while sharing the Hanafi legal school with the Indians, consider all food from the sea to be permissible.

Mediation vs. Inquisition

The focus on the individual in Islamic law gives it a mediatory character (like a mediation process) as opposed to the inquisitorial one of Western law. Unlike the Western system, in which individuals are normally accused by a corporate entity, such as a state or society, whose interests transcend those of the individual, Islamic legal processes traditionally mediate between individuals in which either one party or both parties might accuse the other of a legal transgression.

This function of the judge demands certain interpersonal skills, and it also means that the desired goal of the process is arriving at a settlement, not reaching a verdict. The personal and contextual nature of Islamic law sounds as if it would be fairer than a codified legal system. But critics say that, in practice, the realities of overburdened legal systems and less-than-conscientious judges mean that people who are unfamiliar with the law have fewer safeguards than if they were subject to a rigid legal code.

There's More to Life Than Laws

There is a historical bias in favor of seeing the legal aspects of Islam as the core of the tradition. As a result, Islam is sometimes caricatured as a dry, ritualistic religion that emphasizes legal conformity in one's public behavior over what one believes or does in private. This skewed perspective probably stems from the fact that the ritual and legal aspects of Islam are naturally more visible than personal beliefs, and also from the greater exposure and influence that the practice of law derives from its close relationship with governments, courts, and the police.

In practice, even the most ardent champions of Islamic jurisprudence have seen it as only one facet of their religion. Other scholars have explicitly stated that blind devotion to scholastic traditions of law and philosophy do not represent the core of a fulfilled religious life, and that faith and piety are more important.

The most famous advocate of this viewpoint is al-Ghazali (d. 1111), who spent most of his adult life as a professor of theology. In 1095, while at the height of his professorial career, he suffered a severe emotional crisis that caused him to leave his job in Baghdad and return to his hometown, where he devoted himself to a life of contemplation. He eventually came to the conclusion that rational and philosophical inquiry can carry a person only so far, and that achieving complete understanding requires a leap of faith. This leap of faith was best achieved through mystical training and experience, something commonly referred to as Sufism, which is the topic of the next chapter.

The Least You Need to Know

- After the murder of Uthman (the third Caliph) and the emergence of sectarian divisions in the Islamic world, four major schools of thought emerged, representing the spectrum of Islamic theological opinions.

- By the end of the eighth century, the trends of the four early schools of thought had developed to the point that full-fledged theological schools (Mu'tazila and Ash'ariya) had emerged within the Islamic world.

- Islamic law (Shari'a) is believed to be the collected prescriptions dictated by God for the running of the universe.

- If the Qur'an does not provide clear rules on a question of law, then one looks to the examples of the Prophet Muhammad or his Sunna, and finds an answer by a formal system of reasoning.

Chapter 5

Sufism: Mystical Islam

In This Chapter

- All Muslims will have a direct encounter with God after they die
- The quest for spiritual understanding
- Leadership of the Sufi Orders
- Saints, mystics, and magic

Sufism is an umbrella term for a variety of philosophical, social, and literary phenomena occurring within the Islamic world. In its narrowest sense, the term refers to a number of schools of Islamic mystical philosophy and theology, to religious orders and guilds that have greatly influenced the development of Islamic politics and society, and to the varied expressions of popular piety and shrine-cults found throughout the Islamic world.

In a wider sense, Sufism is often seen as the spiritual muse behind much of pre-modern verse in the Islamic world, the idiom of much of popular

Islamic piety, the primary social arena open to women's religious participation, and a major force in the conversion of people to Islam in Africa and Asia.

Sufi orders served as educational institutions that fostered not only the religious sciences but also music and decorative arts. Sometimes Sufi leaders served as theologians and judges, combining within themselves scholastic and charismatic forms of leadership; at other times, they led the challenge against the legal and theological establishment.

> **On the Right Path**
>
> In modern times (as in other periods in history), the Sufi orders have been praised for their capacity to serve as channels for religious reform. At the same time, they have been criticized for a lack of respect for Islamic law, and for fostering ignorance and superstition in order to maintain their control over the community.

Where Sufism Began

The origins of Sufism lie in a very informal movement of personal piety that emerged in the first century of Islam. These earliest Sufis emphasized prayer, asceticism, and withdrawal from society. The term "Sufism"—or *tasawwuf*, as the tradition is called in Arabic—may derive from the practice of wearing wool (*suf* in Arabic), or possibly from the Arabic word for purity (*safa*). The earliest Sufis spent almost all their waking hours in prayer, and frequently engaged in acts of self-mortification, such as starving themselves or staying up the entire night, as a form of prayer exercise. They renounced their connections to the world and possessed little apart from the clothes on their backs. A large proportion of these early Sufis were women, several of whom, such as Rabi'a al-Adawiya (d. 801), are revered to this day.

It is very likely that the Sufis adopted the practices of asceticism and the wearing of wool after observing the Christian ascetics of Syria and Palestine. Sufis, however, see the origins of their movement in the Qur'an and in the life of Muhammad. They are quick to observe that Muhammad lived an extremely simple, almost ascetic life, and that he had a habit of withdrawing from Mecca to go and meditate in a cave. Indeed, it was while he was meditating in this manner that he received his first revelation. Sufis therefore see their practices as an imitation of Muhammad, and they hope to achieve the same close relationship with God as he did.

Close Encounters of the Direct Kind

According to Islamic belief, all Muslims will have a direct encounter with God after they die (opinions differ as to what this means), but Sufis do not wish to wait that long. This desire is expressed in a saying attributed to the Prophet and which is very popular in Sufi circles that encourages Muslims to "Die before you die."

The direct experience of God is considered so overwhelming as to be inexpressible and can be spoken about only in metaphors. The most commonly used metaphors are those of falling in love and of being intoxicated with wine.

The Sufi concept of union with God is expressed in many different ways. The main problem in Sufi philosophical circles is this: How can a mortal human being unite with the omnipotent, omniscient deity who is unlike us in every way? The union with God is normally called *fana*, which literally means destruction or annihilation. Sufis believe this is the final stage of an individual's spiritual development: She loses any consciousness of her individual identity, and is only aware of the identity of God. In effect, God's identity then replaces the identity of the Sufi.

Muslim Meaning

Fana is a Sufi mystical concept that signifies the annihilation of a person's individuality in the oneness of God.

There is disagreement among Sufis over whether the final spiritual goal of Sufism is to lose one's identity completely in the identity of God, or to reach a stage where one's own petty concerns no longer prevent him or her from seeing the world in its true nature. A common metaphor for the first approach is to describe the Sufi's individuality as a drop that vanishes into the ocean; it does not actually cease to exist, for it is now part of the vastness of the sea; it only ceases to exist as an individual drop.

The latter view, that you see things more clearly, depicts the human heart (considered the seat of the intellect in medieval Islamic thought) as a mirror that is normally dirty, tarnished by one's everyday concerns and petty desires. Through engaging in mystical exercises, a person effectively polishes the mirror of his or her heart and cleanses it to the point where it can accurately reflect the light of God.

The Sufi Path

Sufis believe that average human beings are unable to understand the true nature of spirituality because of their petty concerns. The quest for spiritual understanding in Sufism is seen as a path, which each Sufi must travel under the guidance of a teacher or master. This path has many stages, the number and names of which vary depending on the school of Sufi thought.

In most instances, the first stage on the Sufi path is one of repentance. The Sufi is expected to repent of all the bad deeds he or she has committed in life and to take a vow to avoid all earthly pleasures.

After having repented of the past, the Sufi is supposed to divest him or herself of earthly belongings, which even include attachments to friends and family. In practice, this process of material and emotional divestment is extremely difficult, often takes a long time, and requires strict, meditational exercises under the directions of a master.

Repetition Is the First Law of Learning

The Sufi path relies on meditation called *zikr* (or *dhikr*). At its most basic level, Sufi zikr consists of repeating one of God's names over and over.

Muslim Meaning

Zikr literally means "repetition," "remembrance," "utterance," or "mentioning"; in the Qur'an it appears in the context of urging Muslims to remember their Lord frequently.

In Islam, God is believed to have many names that describe some aspect of his nature. Of these, 99 are considered special and are called the "Most Beautiful Names." The name of God used most frequently in zikr exercises is "Allah" (which Sufis see as the most excellent name), although others, such as *Rahim* (Merciful) or *Wahid* (Unique) are also used. The purpose of reciting these names is to concentrate wholly on what you are doing and to lose all self-awareness. Your entire being becomes permeated with the zikr formula through repetition, so that even if you cease actively to engage in zikr, it continues to be repeated in your heart.

Waiting to Exhale

Some zikr exercises involve the repetition of longer formulas, while others also entail complicated methods of breathing control. An example of a relatively simple zikr exercise involving breathing control requires the Sufi to say out loud a bisyllabic name of God (such as "Wahid," meaning "The Unique"), inhaling on the first syllable and exhaling on the second.

This practice is called the "Sawing zikr," because the distinctive sound made by speaking while inhaling and then while exhaling resembles the noise made by a saw as it cuts through wood. Other forms of zikr are much more complicated, such as one that involves reciting the formula "There is no god but God" in a long breath broken up into five beats.

On the Right Path

Some older, complex meditational exercises were very difficult to learn on one's own, and only became popular after the master-disciple relationship had evolved to the point that Sufis were organized into hierarchical Sufi orders, called *tariqas*.

Organized Sufism

By the thirteenth century, Islamic educational and legal institutions had been formalized, as had the relationship between the government and theological and legal scholars. It is therefore no surprise that Sufism would also take an organized form and compete for social legitimacy and authority with other religious movements and institutions.

The earliest Sufi orders were made up of the disciples of a particular master; after these disciples had themselves become accomplished Sufis, they imparted their master's teachings to their own students. So began the tradition of students obeying the teachings of an initial master, and following his *Tariqa* (path), an organizational system that became formalized by the fifteenth century.

Bet You Didn't Know

Before an aspirant Sufi could join an order or Tariqa, he would often be turned away repeatedly to test his sincerity, or forced to perform menial tasks as a process of initiation. Admission into an order was normally a ceremonial occasion, when new members would be given robes signifying their new status.

Many Sufi orders have been extremely important in the evolution of Islamic society. Not only did they have prominent scholars and philosophers developing their ideas, but frequently major figures in the government belonged to these orders. This meant that Sufi orders could influence the official policies of the kingdom. Three such orders deserve special attention: Chishti, Mevlevi, and Naqshbandi; each will be described in the sections that follow.

The Chishti Order

The Chishti order takes its name from Khaja Mu'in al-Din Chishti (d. 1235), who came from a town in Afghanistan and settled in the city of Ajmer in India, where he taught a large number of influential disciples. These disciples opened Chishti centers in provincial towns all over India; they also had many rulers, princes, and princesses as their disciples, and rapidly became the most influential order in India. The Chishti order has as its zikr a particular kind of musical performance called *Qawwali*, in which a group of musicians sing religious songs set to a very rhythmic beat.

Bet You Didn't Know

The late Pakistani singer, Nusrat Fateh Ali Khan (d. 1997), whose fame spread to the West, was the best-known modern exponent of the Qawwali.

The Mevlevi Order

The Mevlevi order is largely limited to the Turkish and Balkan areas of the Ottoman Empire (thirteenth to early twentieth century). Its members became well known in Europe as the "Whirling Dervishes," on account of their distinctive zikr ritual. The order derives its name from the famous mystical poet Jalal al-Din Rumi (d. 1273), called Mevlana in Turkish. Rumi was born in Central Asia and moved to Turkey in 1219, where his father was appointed a professor of legal thought in Konya, the seat of the rulers of that time. Rumi inherited this post after his father's death. In 1244, he fell under the spell of a wandering mystic named Shams-e Tabrizi, and after the latter's mysterious disappearance, Rumi devoted himself to the guidance of Sufi disciples and the writing of poetry.

A distinctive feature of the Mevlevi order is the importance given to music and dance in their zikr practices. The Mevlevi meditational exercise, called *sema*, involves the recitation of prayers and hymns, after which the participants make several rounds of the hall, in a dance with their arms extended sideways, the right palm facing upward and the left downward, and whirl counterclockwise, using their left feet as a pivot. The sema symbolizes the simultaneous receipt of divine grace and its transmission to humanity. The Mevlevi order has emphasized art and culture since Rumi's day, and has inspired both court poets in Ottoman times and young musicians and poets in modern Turkey.

The Naqshbandi Order

Unlike the Mevlevi and Chishti orders, which are both geographically and ethnically limited in range,

the Naqshbandi order is distributed widely throughout the Islamic world. It is named after a Central
Asian Sufi scholar from the city of Bukhara in Uzbekistan named Baha al-Din Naqshband (d. 1389).
Naqshbandis believe that Sufis should not withdraw
from society but should pursue their spiritual goals
while fulfilling all their social responsibilities. They
hold eight principles to be central to their order:

- Awareness while breathing
- Watching your steps
- Journeying within
- Solitude within human society
- Recollection
- Restraining your thoughts
- Watching your thoughts
- Concentration on the Divine

Naqshbandi figures were very important in religious
reform movements in the eighteenth and nineteenth
centuries, particularly in India and Central Asia
where Muslims were fighting British and Russian
colonialism, respectively. In the twentieth century, a
whole host of Naqshbandi groups encouraged the
Turkish-speaking subject peoples of the Soviet
Union to resist Russian domination.

Today, many Naqshbandis provide education and
social services in the Central Asian and Caucasian
countries that emerged after the Soviet Union's
collapse. In recent years, one branch of the Naqshbandis has become active in Muslim circles in the

United States and Europe. Their supporters welcome their apolitical stress on piety and religious tolerance; their critics see them as undermining the Islamic emphasis on individual empowerment by concentrating on the cult of personality surrounding the Sufi master.

Veneration of Saints

One of the most frequent criticisms leveled against Sufism is that most Sufi practice elevates individual shaykhs (or pirs, as Sufi masters are often called in non-Arab societies) to a superhuman level, accords them miraculous powers, and encourages ordinary people to devote themselves entirely to these masters. Despite the fact that many strict interpretations of Islam reject the notion that any class of human beings has the power to intercede with God on behalf of ordinary Muslims, the overwhelming majority of Muslims believe in and venerate saints in a variety of ways.

There are two main types of saints:

- Members of Muhammad's family, whose shrines are visited by both Shi'is and Sunnis, who hold the family of Muhammad in high regard.

- Important Sufi figures whose shrines become famous at a local or regional level as a place where prayers have a good chance of being answered.

On the Right Path

An example of a local saint would be Telli Baba (literally, "Father Tinsel"), whose shrine, situated just to the north of Istanbul, Turkey, is visited by women looking for a husband. The strange name of the shrine derives from the pieces of tinsel that cover the tomb. Visitors take a piece of tinsel from the shrine, and when their wishes are granted they return with an offering of money and a handful of tinsel to add to the tomb.

Innumerable local shrines can be found across the Islamic world. Other Sufi shrines have an international importance and are visited by millions of people, particularly on festivals that commemorate the birth or death of the saint. These include the shrine of Mu'in al-Din Chishti in Ajmer, India, and Sayyida Zaynab (the great, great, great granddaughter of the Prophet) in Cairo.

The key ingredient in the charisma of a saint is the possession of a quality called *baraka*, a miraculous power that is bestowed on human beings by God. Baraka gives its possessors curative and mediatory powers, enabling them not only to intercede before God on behalf of their devotees but also to solve social, economic, physical, and spiritual problems. It functions as an almost physical commodity and is contagious inasmuch as it is normally passed from a saint to his or her descendants or to a designated successor.

> ### Muslim Meaning
>
> **Baraka** (sometimes barkat or bereket) is a miraculous power bestowed on human beings by God, and is believed to be possessed by Sufi saints.

For the most part, however, baraka is transmitted only within families; a saint's successor who is not a blood relative is normally understood to have possessed "latent" baraka that was brought to the fore by association with the saint. Followers or devotees of a saint make humble prayers and offerings in order to acquire some of his baraka, although the kind they possess is not contagious; in other words, baraka rubs off from a saint onto individual followers, but this baraka never gets translated into their own and cannot be transferred to others.

Mysticism and Magic

Magic is an awkward concept for many Muslims, for it implies that supernatural powers do not ultimately derive from God—a clearly heretical stance. Nonetheless, magic does undeniably permeate the lives of many Muslims for whom a world without jinn (demonic beings) and magical powers is inconceivable.

For instance, within clear sight of an affluent section of the Moroccan capital of Rabat stand the ruins of the Phoenician city of Sala, where, sandwiched between an egret rookery and a clump of banana trees, lies a square pond of pre-Islamic design. The pond contains a colony of eels that are fed eggs by visiting women as an aid to conceiving a child. Next to the pond are a number of Islamic tombs from the fourteenth-century Merenid period, the presence of which establishes a direct link between the offerings made at the pond and the curative powers of these shrines.

In the Mediterranean and west Asian worlds, most magical practices engaged in by Muslims are to ward off the "evil eye." Belief in the evil eye is integrally linked with people's understanding of the Qur'an; the short, final three chapters are frequently recited for the express purpose of warding off the evil eye, and people commonly recite certain other verses of the Qur'an, wear talismans made out of them, or ritualistically consume or burn them. The preparation and acquisition of talismans is strongly associated with Sufi shrines, and there is a direct correlation between the potency accorded to a talisman and the reputation as a miracle worker, or the baraka, of the person providing it.

At first glance, mystical traditions of Islam seem to be disparate and lacking in any overlapping functions and concerns. Throughout Islamic history, prominent scholars of theology have also been renowned as respected mystics. In addition, masters of a Sufi order have functioned as respected mystics (and as the legal authorities in their communities). This lack of rigid delineation between religious specializations has allowed for the easier integration of the intellectual tradition into everyday life.

The next chapter will talk about the highly developed Muslim rituals and beliefs.

The Least You Need to Know

- Sufis served as educators, theologians, and judges, combining within themselves scholastic and charismatic forms of leadership; at other times, they led the challenge against the legal and theological establishment.

- According to Islamic belief, all Muslims will have a direct encounter with God after they die, but Sufis express this desire in a saying attributed to the Prophet and very popular in Sufi circles that encourages Muslims to "Die before you die."

- The quest for spiritual understanding in Sufism is seen as a path (consisting of many stages), which each Sufi must travel under the guidance of a teacher or master.

- The earliest Sufi orders were made up of the disciples of a particular master; after these disciples had themselves become accomplished Sufis, they imparted their master's teachings to their own students.

- The two main types of saints are members of Muhammad's family (their shrines are visited by both Shi'is and Sunnis) and important Sufi figures whose shrines become famous at a local or regional level as a place where prayers have a good chance of being answered.

Pillars of the Faith

In This Chapter

- Tawhid and the oneness of God
- God wishes to communicate with human beings
- Angels exist and perform God's will
- The world will end and you will be judged
- Here are your rites

Muslims have a number of highly developed rituals and beliefs, all of which are seen as having their basis in the Qur'an and the life of Muhammad. They were further developed by legal scholars and theologians at different times and in different cultural contexts, which may explain why there is so much variation in observance of rituals, and even in Muslims' understanding of the fundamental texts of the faith.

Muslims believe in five cardinal points, which are so central to the religion that they are called the "Pillars of Faith": These are Divine Unity, Prophecy, Revelation, Angelic Agency, and the existence of an Afterlife.

Most of the rituals and doctrines outlined in this chapter are those of the Sunni sect, which accounts for the overwhelming majority of Muslims, although even the Sunnis have some differences. These are most striking in practices surrounding birth, marriage, and other festivals marking passage through life; however, they are also apparent in the practice of rituals, such as prayer.

Divine Unity

Muslims believe in the oneness of God, a concept known by its Arabic name, *tawhid*. The term tawhid not only refers to the concept of God's unity but also to the affirmation of this unity by human beings. In other words, the notion of tawhid makes human beings active participants in ensuring that God remains understood as a unique being and thus crucial actors in God's relationship with the world.

The unique nature of God is frequently attested to in the Qur'an. Two short sections of the scripture are particularly valuable in providing a general understanding of how God is viewed by the majority of Muslims.

The first of these constitutes a very brief chapter in its entirety and is called "Sincerity" (*Ikhlas*, Chapter 112):

> Say, He is God, the One and Only
> God, the Eternal, Absolute;
> He begets not, nor is He begotten;
> And there is none like unto Him.

The second is a single verse in a much longer chapter (Chapter 2, verse 255):

> God! There is no God but Him, the Living, the Eternal. No slumber can seize Him nor sleep. His are all things in the heavens and on Earth. Who is there can intercede in His presence except as He permits? He knows what is before them and what after [or behind] them. Nor shall they compass aught of his knowledge except as He wills. His throne extends over the heavens and the earth, and He feels no fatigue in guarding and preserving them, for He is the Most High, the Supreme [in glory].

On the Right Path

According to Islamic understanding, God has no body and is unlike anything in the created world. Furthermore, it is a very grave sin to consider anything as an equal or companion of God. There has been, nonetheless, a substantial debate among Muslim theologians and philosophers over whether or not God is similar enough to human beings for us to be able to use anthropomorphic language to describe him.

As is clearly emphasized by these selections from the Qur'an, God is unique and eternal. He exists in and of himself and has no needs. For reasons that are inscrutable to human beings, God created the universe and all that exists within it; he created human beings and gave them the capacity to do good as well as evil, and the ability to choose between the two. Human beings can know God through his attributes (such as mercy, justice, compassion, wrath, and so on), but the ultimate essence of God remains unknowable.

Prophecy

Muslims are supposed to believe that God wishes to communicate with human beings, and that he uses prophets for this purpose. Prophets are of two types, the first being those who have a mission from God to warn their communities and acquaint them with God's will; these are referred to as *anbiya* (singular: nabi). The second category, in addition to fulfilling all the functions of the first group, is also given a revealed scripture that is supposed to be conveyed to their community. This special category of anbiya is called *rusul* (singular: *rasul*, meaning "messenger").

Muslims believe in a series of prophets that includes all the prophets mentioned in the Hebrew Bible as well as Jesus and Muhammad. The belief in Muhammad's role as the last prophet has emerged as a key tenet of Islamic dogma and is used as an important yardstick by which Islamic orthodoxy is judged.

At times, the emphasis on the finality of Muhammad's prophecy seems to be primarily semantic, since Shi'i beliefs grant the Imam a religious role that often appears more important than that of any prophet; yet, the majority of Sunnis continue to regard Shi'is as Muslims.

Muslims consider Jesus to have been the second last prophet, who foretold the coming of Muhammad. The majority of Sunnis also consider Jesus to be the messiah and believe in the Virgin Birth. They do not, however, take this to mean that God was Jesus' father, but rather that God performed a miracle by causing Mary to conceive without a biological father.

Revelation

Muslims believe that God uses his prophets to reveal scriptures to humanity. Four such scriptures are recognized: the Torah as revealed to Moses, the Psalms of David, the Gospel of Jesus, and the Qur'an of Muhammad. According to Muslim belief, God's message is eternal and the substance of all these books is therefore the same.

Differences between them are either explained by the fact that, after their revelation, earlier scriptures were tampered with by people who claimed to believe in them, or else by using a concept of human evolution. According to this theory, God always knew what he wished to teach humanity; however, humanity was not always ready for the full message. For this reason, God revealed his message in progressively more comprehensive versions, culminating in the Qur'an, which is the definitive version of God's message, valid until the end of civilization.

Bet You Didn't Know

Scripture is central to the Muslim understanding of religion; Jews and Christians are therefore referred to as "People of the Book" (Ahl al-kitab), and their religions are recognized as divinely sanctioned.

Angelic Agency

Muslims are supposed to believe that angels exist and that they are used by God to perform his will. One of their duties is to watch over individual human beings and keep a record of all their actions. The most famous angel is Gabriel, who served as an intermediary between God and Muhammad in the revelation of the Qur'an. Another important figure is Iblis, who used to be the chief of all angels but was punished for disobeying God by being cast out of heaven. After that, he was turned into Satan and now not only rules hell but also tries to tempt human beings from the path of goodness.

Many Muslims consider belief in angels to be the most difficult of the Pillars of Faith and explain them away as natural forces or different aspects of God's power. Others, however, have a complex belief in a variety of supernatural beings including angels and demons (normally but not exclusively called *Jinn*), who interact with human beings in different ways, both malevolent and therapeutic.

Judgment and Afterlife

Muslims believe that our world will eventually come to an end and that we will be judged and rewarded or punished in the afterlife according to our actions on Earth. Judgment, reward, and punishment are central points in Islam and are the foundation upon which its entire system of ethics is based.

It is therefore no surprise that Islam has a highly developed theory of the end of the world.

According to popular belief, the coming of doomsday is foretold by a number of signs similar to those found in the Book of Revelations: a struggle between good and evil, the changed rising of the sun, the sounding of a trumpet, and the appearance of a beast. When things reach their darkest point a Messiah returns and gathers up all virtuous people to await doomsday and resurrection.

On the Right Path

It is important to note that, according to the Qur'an, the world does not so much come to a complete end as it is utterly transformed. It is therefore easy to argue that the afterlife occurs right here and not in some other place (in other words, heaven is not necessarily somewhere above us).

After the end of the world, all human beings who have ever lived will be resurrected and judged. Some Muslims believe that this resurrection is only spiritual and that we will not be restored to our physical bodies. At judgment, we will stand face to face with God for the first time and will be expected to answer for our actions. Those completely free from sin will go directly to heaven. Others will have to spend time in hell to pay for their sins before they enter heaven to live eternally.

Islam does not have a strong concept of eternal damnation in hell; the time people spend there depends on the degree to which they have sinned. The only category of people who will stay in hell forever are religious hypocrites, those who claim to be Muslims but are not. This kind of hypocrisy is regarded as such a great sin that no amount of punishment can adequately pay for it.

The Qur'an paints an extremely vivid picture of heaven as a garden with streams and fruit trees, where the dead live a lavish and comfortable life. Many Muslims take this picture of heaven literally. Others see it as a metaphor for a state of spiritual bliss, where the greatest reward will be living closely with God.

Life-cycle Rites

Islamic societies the world over practice a number of rites to mark each individual's path through life from birth to death. Most of these rites differ markedly in their details from one society to the next. There are, however, certain turning points in human life that are particularly emphasized as Islamic religious events and which, at some basic level, are observed in similar ways. Three of these life-cycle rites are the circumcision of male children, marriage, and death and funerary customs.

This Won't Hurt a Bit

Male circumcision is not mentioned in the Qur'an but the practice is believed to be essential in all Islamic societies. Hadith describes it as a custom practiced by all prophets before Muhammad and particularly by Abraham, who is said to have circumcised himself at the age of 80. Muslim boys are circumcised from early infancy until the onset of puberty, depending on the culture to which they belong and the social class of their parents.

Bet You Didn't Know

In many Islamic communities, the ideal age for circumcision is seven days because tradition states that Muhammad performed the ritual on his grandchildren, Hasan and Husayn, when they were one week old. In other contexts the age is 10 years, because another hadith says that the Prophet's cousin, Ibn Abbas, was circumcised at that age.

For many urban families, the rite is performed on an infant in a hospital or clinic and is accompanied by very little fanfare. For others, it occurs as part of a major ceremony and is a rite of passage that is remembered by the boy on whom it is performed.

This is particularly true of Malaysia and Turkey, where circumcision usually occurs around the age of 13. The boy is dressed as a prince and, depending on the financial means of the family, an elaborate feast takes place after the ceremony, at which time the boy receives a large number of gifts. In these societies, the circumcision serves as a puberty rite that marks a boy's passage into adulthood. The public nature of the ceremony enables him to show his bravery and honor; after this ceremony, he is considered a full member of Islamic society and is expected to pray and fast like an adult.

A Stroll Down the Aisle

Marriage is a basic component of Muslim social life, and though not explicitly listed as a religious duty, many people consider it as such and view a celibate or monastic life as somehow inferior and incomplete. Their justification for this view lies in the frequent references to marriage in the Qur'an as well as in the custom of the Prophet Muhammad, who was married himself.

The Prophet reportedly said that there should be no celibacy in Islam, and that when a person gets married, they fulfill half of their religious obligations. The Qur'an contains extensive rules concerning who you are permitted to marry and what constitutes the rights and duties of a husband and wife. Details that are not found in the Qur'an are filled in from the Sunna of the Prophet and the living customs of each society.

Muhammad grew up in an extremely patriarchal society, where almost all economic and social power rested with men. The new Islamic laws of Qur'an, by contrast, explicitly listed many new rights that women could demand of men. Muslim feminists and liberal theologians often agree that many of these rules seem archaic or unfair when viewed from the perspective of modern Western society. Yet, it is important to note that they constituted important reforms in the legal status of women at the time they were introduced.

According to Sunni Islamic law, a man can marry either a Muslim woman or one who belongs to another monotheistic religion. A woman, on the other hand, can only marry a Muslim man. This inequality derives from a viewpoint that sees the primary purpose for getting married as providing an appropriate environment for raising children. The patriarchal social system that has represented an ideal in most Islamic societies expects children to follow the religion of their father and expects the offspring of a Muslim mother and a non-Muslim father to be lost to the Muslim community. Shi'i law is even stricter on this issue and does not permit a Shi'i man to marry a non-Muslim woman.

Islamic law also permits a man to marry up to four wives at one time. However, the Qur'an encourages him to treat each of them perfectly equally and, in the very same chapter, states that this is impossible to do. Muslims opposed to polygamy see these verses of the Qur'an as an implicit outlawing of the practice, which, they believe, was only permitted as a temporary measure because pre-Islamic Arab men were used to having many wives and would not accept a sudden change in their marital customs.

The Qur'an stipulates categories of relatives re-ferred to as *mahram* ("forbidden" or "sacrosanct"), who, by reason of particular degrees of affinity or blood, a person cannot marry. In practical terms, the only difference with common Western practices is that it is permissible to marry one's first cousin. In many traditional societies, this is the preferred form of marriage, because it not only reinforces family bonds but also makes sure that property remains within the extended family.

Bet You Didn't Know

In everyday life, the concept of mahram relationships is most relevant in communities and families where female veiling is prevalent, since women are not supposed to appear unveiled before a non-mahram male.

In its barest essence, the Islamic institution of marriage is a legal, contractual arrangement that provides a materially secure environment for children to grow up in and a socially acceptable outlet for sexual desire. The letter of the law sees marriage as nothing more than this; therefore, it concentrates on the details of entering into the contract and makes provisions for breaking it in the event of divorce. However, every Islamic culture attaches great importance to the marriage ceremony and buries the legal parts of the ceremony in an ornate series of celebrations. Many of these marriage customs are primarily cultural: A Syrian Muslim ceremony is very similar to a Syrian Christian one, just as an Indian Muslim wedding shares a great deal with a Hindu one.

The legal core of the Islamic marriage ceremony involves the signing and witnessing of the marriage contract. This contract can be signed either by the bride and groom or else by their guardians. An important aspect of the contract is the fixing of a "bride price," which is given by the groom to the bride and becomes her personal wealth. In some cultures, the bride price is a promissory note, and serves as a strong disincentive for men to initiate divorce; in others, it is considered little more than a formality or quaint custom. Nevertheless, the fact that it persists is seen by its critics as a glaring symbol of women's continued status as a commodity that a husband acquires in marriage.

The Islamic laws concerning marriage allow for the possibility of divorce. It is legally easier for a husband to divorce his wife than the other way around, although there are clear provisions through which a woman can sue for divorce in the event of abuse, neglect, or abandonment. Nevertheless, most Islamic societies continue to be socially conservative and family oriented, and even though divorce is legally permissible, there is enormous social pressure against it.

Death (and the Funeral)

Muslims view death as the culmination of life, at which time human beings return to God and answer for their actions in this world. As a result, just as it is by members of many other religions, death is viewed by Muslims as a passage from one sort of life to the next.

Ideally, Muslims should die facing the direction of the Ka'ba in Mecca and with the *Shahada* ("There is no god but Allah and Muhammad is the messenger of Allah") on their lips. Those who are too weak to do so themselves are assisted by relatives, who recite the Shahada for them. In many societies, people also recite the thirty-sixth chapter of the Qur'an, entitled Ya-Sin, which contains several powerful verses dealing with the subject of death.

A person is supposed to be buried within a day of their death; one who dies in the morning should be buried before nightfall, and one who dies in the evening should be buried the next morning. In practice, burials are often delayed by several days when, for example, an individual dies while away from home and has to be brought back for burial.

The corpse is ritually bathed before death, a task that is traditionally performed by family members who belong to the same sex as the deceased. This washing follows the same form as the ritual ablutions performed before prayer, except that the body is washed an odd number of times (usually three) using soap and water, which is sometimes perfumed. There is no tradition among Muslims of embalming, dressing, or adorning the body. The body is wrapped unclothed in a white cotton shroud, which covers it from head to toe. Coffins are not normally used, but when they are, they are made of very simple materials.

The only acceptable way of disposing of a body in the eyes of most Muslims is through burial under ground. The grave is approximately 5 feet deep with an alcove carved out at the bottom (so that the grave has an L-shaped cross-section). The body is placed in this alcove resting on its right side with the head facing Mecca. The alcove is then closed up (sometimes with unfired clay bricks) and the grave filled in.

Strict interpretations of Islamic law do not allow the construction of permanent graves; instead, they require graves to be simple mounds of dirt with perhaps a modest headstone marking the site. In practice, a long-standing tradition exists of making elaborate graves in all parts of the Islamic world, and some of the innumerable mausoleums of saints and aristocrats rank among the masterpieces of Islamic architecture.

On the Right Path

The Taj Mahal in Agra, India, is an example of a tomb, as is the Mamluk necropolis in Cairo, Egypt. In some places, entire cities have grown around the tomb of a highly respected religious person, such as those of Karbala in Iraq, Mashhad in Iran, and Mazar-e Sharif in Afghanistan.

Islamic burial is traditionally marked by a simple funeral service. Traditionally, four men carry the funeral bier to the cemetery. The bier itself is usually a modest cot with a white or green sheet shrouding the body. Joining in a funeral procession is considered a collective duty: If there are not enough people accompanying the body to the cemetery, then individual Muslims are duty-bound to join in, although in the busy streets of modern cities, the observance of this rule is increasingly rare.

The funeral prayer is a variation on the Muslim Salat or ritual prayer, although the funerary service also includes several prayers for the deceased, asking for the person to be guided and forgiven in the afterlife. An interesting anomaly in Islamic rites concerning death and burial involves the treatment of children and martyrs: Since small children are not believed to be accountable for their actions, the funeral prayer does not include a plea for forgiveness on their behalf. Similarly, martyrs are believed to be absolved of all sins; not only does one not ask for the forgiveness of their sins, but they are also not bathed before burial; they are to be buried in the clothes they were wearing when they died.

Many societies have set days after the burial (especially the fortieth day) when special rituals are performed to remember the deceased. These normally involve the distribution of food or money among the needy and the gathering of mourners to read the Qur'an. Individual and collective wailing (especially by women) is also fairly common despite many injunctions against it in Islamic legal writings.

The Least You Need to Know

- Muslims believe in the oneness of God (tawhid), which also refers to the affirmation of this unity by human beings—making them active participants in ensuring that God remains understood as a unique being.

- Muslims believe that God uses his prophets to reveal scriptures to humanity: the Torah of Moses, the Psalms of David, the Gospel of Jesus, and the Qur'an of Muhammad.

- Muslims believe that our world will eventually come to an end and that we will be judged and rewarded or punished in the afterlife according to our actions on Earth.

- Islamic societies practice a number of rites to mark each individual's path through life.

Pillars of Practice

In This Chapter

- Professing faith
- When and how to pray
- Fasting and charity
- Pilgrimage
- Striving in the path of God

There are certain ritual practices that are required of all pious Muslims. These are the *Shahada*, Prayer, Fasting, giving Charity, and the Hajj pilgrimage. Even though they recognize the importance of these rituals, many Muslims do not observe all of them, or they observe them only partially. Islamic law provides extensive guidelines on the circumstances under which someone is not obligated to engage in ritual and on how one makes up for ritual responsibilities that he or she has missed.

> ### Muslim Meaning
>
> **Shahada** is the Islamic profession of faith (refer to the section "Shahada"): "I bear witness that there is no god except the God and I bear witness that Muhammad is the messenger of God!"

It is very important to make a formal intention to engage in a ritual before actually doing it, otherwise the ritual obligation will not have been fulfilled. For example, Muslims are obligated to donate a percentage of their wealth in a form of charity called *zakat*. If you were to give away money without first making the conscious intention of fulfilling your zakat obligation, it would still be a good deed but would not count as zakat.

> ### Muslim Meaning
>
> **Zakat** is the ritual of alms-giving, which consists of giving a fixed percentage of your wealth in charity every year (refer to the section "Alms-Giving").

The Call to Prayer

The Islamic call to prayer, or *adhan*, is one of the most distinctive features of any Muslim societal landscape—five times a day, a human voice rings out, marking the time for prayer. In most cultures the sound is musical, while in parts of Africa it is consciously not so, but everywhere the Arabic words are instantly recognizable for what they are:

> God is Greatest! God is Greatest! God is Greatest! God is Greatest! I witness that there is no god but God! I witness that there is no god but God! I witness that Muhammad is the messenger of God! I witness that Muhammad is the messenger of God! Come to prayer! Come to prayer! Come to salvation! Come to salvation! God is Greatest! God is Greatest! There is no god but God!

Muslim Meaning

Adhan is the Islamic call to prayer (sometimes called *azan*). It is broadcast from mosques five times a day.

The adhan is delivered shortly before the times of the five daily ritual prayers, which can be performed in a mosque—a building dedicated to the purpose— or, as is practiced more frequently, at home. Like members of other religious communities, the majority of Muslims are not strict observers of religious ritual and pray somewhat irregularly. But even for those Muslims who pray infrequently, the adhan marks the passage of time through the day (in much the same way as church bells do in many Christian communities) and serves as a constant re- minder that they are living in a Muslim community. Equally important, the Arabic that is used for the adhan directly evokes a connection to the Qur'an, the Islamic scripture that is believed by Muslims to be God's literal word, and thereby reaffirms God's continual presence in human life.

Prayer and the Mosque

The ritual prayer, called *salat*, is supposed to be performed five times a day, at set periods (following the adhan), and in a prescribed manner. Although most Muslims do not observe this ritual with such regularity, they do consider salat to be a central aspect of their religion and associate its performance with piety. There are a variety of other forms of Muslim prayer, such as personal, informal prayers in which one asks something of God, or mystical prayers that help attain some sort of spiritual advancement. Salat's status as a fundamental ritual sets it apart from these other forms and places it at the heart of Islamic religious life.

Muslim Meaning

Salat is the name of the Islamic ritual prayer. In most languages, other than Arabic, it is called *namaz*. Refer to the section that follows "Prayer" for more specifics.

During salat, worshipers kneel and place their foreheads on the floor as a symbol of their total submission to the will of God (known as *sajda*, or prostration). Some people proudly bear a callous mark in the middle of their foreheads as a symbol of a lifetime of prayer. The sajda's importance is obvious from the fact that an Islamic house of prayer (the equivalent of a church or synagogue) is called a *masjid*, or "place of doing the sajda." Through Spanish, masjid has made its way into English as the word "mosque."

Muslims are not required to go to the mosque in order to perform their ritual prayers but are encouraged to do so, particularly in the case of the midday prayer on Fridays (designated as the weekly congregational prayer) and for the special prayers offered on major religious holidays.

On the Right Path

Major mosques, such as the massive Suleymaniye Mosque in Istanbul, Turkey, serve as the focal point of entire towns or quarters of large cities. Built in the sixteenth century, the Suleymaniye sits at the center of a large complex that included a hospital, public kitchens, an orphanage, and educational institutions, called **madrasas,** which taught religious and scientific studies. At a more abstract level, the complex symbolized an Islamic model of the world and the values that are considered important within it.

Mosques vary tremendously in size, architectural style, and wealth of ornamentation; they can be as simple as a courtyard with a mark on the wall to indicate the direction of prayer (called the *qibla*), or imposing cathedral-like buildings that dominate a city's skyline and represent the pinnacle of architectural expertise in their society. Most commonly, mosques contain a source of water for people to perform their ablutions (ritual washing) prior to prayer; a niche—called *mihrab*—which marks the direction of the qibla; and a pulpit—called a *minbar*—which is used for sermons, lectures, and general announcements.

Muslim Meaning

The **mihrab** (niche) is an artistic focal point of the mosque. State- or imperially funded congregational mosques have stunning mihrabs of tilework or inlay of the most ornate kind. **Minbars** (pulpits) can be fixed or movable in the mosque and are frequently made of ornately carved wood or stone.

The atmosphere in most mosques tends to be relaxed and informal. They contain little furniture (since Muslims pray on the ground) and, in societies relatively free of crime or sectarian violence, are kept unlocked. It is not uncommon to find people sitting in small groups inside a mosque engaging in informal prayers or casual conversation, or simply taking a break from the heat of the day or the crowded streets.

Bearing Witness: Shahada

Shahada literally means "witnessing" and is a shorter form of the term *Kalimat al-shahada*, the statement of bearing witness that forms the credal formula of Islam. The statement literally translates as: "I bear witness that there is no god except the God and I bear witness that Muhammad is the messenger of God!"

This formula is often broken into its components in order to show what the central beliefs of Islam are, especially the nature of the Islamic understanding of God. The whole formula is framed as an affirmation or assertion; in other words, it is supposed to be a voluntary and conscious declaration of your beliefs.

- Uttering the first half of the Shahada ("... there is no god except the God) makes a person a monotheist but not necessarily a Muslim; it is something that could be said just as faithfully by Christians or Jews.
- The second half of the formula ("... Muhammad is the messenger of God!") distinguishes Muslims from other monotheists, because belief in the finality of Muhammad's prophetic mission is what sets Muslims apart from followers of other religions.

The Shahada so perfectly encapsulates the essence of Islamic faith that it is often referred to as the foundation stone on which the Pillars of Faith and Pillars of Practice stand. It is the first thing that is whispered into a baby's ears when she is born, and it is the utterance that Muslims try to have on their lips at the moment of death. It is also the formula by which someone converts to Islam—many people believe that simply uttering the Shahada makes one a Muslim.

Prayer: Salat

Sunnis and Twelver Shi'is (dominant in Iran), who together account for the overwhelming majority of all Muslims, are ritually required to pray five times a day. This kind of prayer, called Salat in Arabic and Namaz in many other languages, is very formal and ritualistic, and is not to be confused with the informal, private prayer that most Muslims engage in anytime they feel like asking God for something or when simply conversing with him.

Salat prayers are performed just before daybreak, just after the sun has reached the highest point in the sky, in the middle of the afternoon, just after sunset, and after dark. It is worth noting that although all the prayers are linked to the sun, none of them is performed precisely at the moment of a sun-related time (for example, at sunrise or sunset). This is consciously to disassociate Islam from any form of sun worship.

Muslims are not required to pray communally, although it is considered better to pray with other people when possible since this helps strengthen social bonds. You can pray at home or anywhere else, as long as the place is not unclean. Cleanliness is more a matter of ritual purity than of hygiene, although an obviously filthy place (such as a sewer or public restroom) is not appropriate for prayer. Ritually impure places are normally associated with death, be it human or animal (for example, a slaughterhouse).

Before prayer, a person is supposed to perform the ritual called *wudu* (or wuzu), which involves washing one's hands, face, and feet in a prescribed way. Once again, this is a "ritual" purification rather than a matter of hygiene. No soap is used, and when water is unavailable, one can simply go through the motions of washing them with "dry" hands. After entering such a state of ritual purity, the Muslim stands facing Mecca and makes the formal intention to pray.

On the Right Path

Salat prayers consist of a set of Qur'anic verses that are recited in a cycle of standing, sitting, and kneeling positions. Each cycle is called a rak'a, the number of which varies according to which of the daily prayers is being performed.

There is little latitude in what one says during the salat; the majority of verses or phrases are set, being derived from the Qur'an. There are certain points in each cycle when the individual Muslim can select a passage from the Qur'an to recite, but he or she cannot choose anything else to incorporate into the prayer (that is, a non-Qur'anic prayer or hymn). Furthermore, the salat prayers are always to be performed in Arabic, even by those Muslims (the majority of the population worldwide) who do not understand the language. As such, salat is not prayer in the sense of a personal conversation with God but rather a ritual obligation that must be fulfilled to reaffirm one's relationship with God.

Fasting: During Ramadan

Muslims are supposed to fast during the month of *Ramadan*, the ninth month of the Islamic lunar calendar. The fast consists of abstaining from eating, drinking, smoking, violence, and engaging in sex from before sunrise until after sunset for the entire month. Not only are you supposed to refrain from these things but also from thinking about them. Going hungry and thirsty and avoiding violent or sexual thoughts is supposed to teach self-awareness, and also make one more sympathetic toward those who are less fortunate—those who not only have to go without food and water through necessity, but also who have to hide their anger and desire because they always live at the mercy of others.

Ramadan is the holiest month of the Islamic year, and fasting is one of the most social of Islamic rituals. In countries with an Islamic majority, the entire daily schedule changes during Ramadan to accommodate the fast. Most families wake up before sunrise to eat a substantial breakfast and to pray. The beginning of the fast is either announced by a siren ballast or else by men who walk through the streets beating a drum.

Muslim Meaning

Ramadan is the ninth month of the Islamic lunar calendar, during which practicing Muslims fast, abstaining from eating, drinking, smoking, violence, and sex from before sunrise until after sunset for the entire month.

Restaurants either close completely during the day or else are very discreet about serving customers. In some conservative societies it is illegal to eat or drink in public, and only certain restaurants are allowed to stay open in order to feed non-Muslims or travelers. Many Muslims break the fast in a simple way by drinking water and eating either some salt or a few dates, in imitation of Muhammad's practice. Supper tends to be more lavish than it would be at other times of the year. The entire month has a festive atmosphere combined with a great sense of piety. Children often insist on fasting, because the practice is associated with growing up; the first time a child is allowed by his or her parents to fast for a whole day or for the entire month is a major event in many Muslims' lives and serves as an informal rite of passage.

Alms-giving: Zakat

The giving of charity is considered an extremely meritorious act in Islam. Just as in the case of prayer, a particular kind of alms-giving is differentiated from others because it is done ritually. Known as zakat, it consists of giving away a certain percentage of one's wealth in charity. The percentage given away varies by sect, ranging from 2.5 percent among Sunnis to 10 percent in some Shi'i groups. There is also a great deal of variation in what forms of wealth and income are considered taxable for zakat; for example, whether or not income (as opposed to assets) is taxable, and in how one calculates the tax for agricultural products.

In some modern Islamic societies, the zakat tax is collected by the government in the same way as other taxes. This tax income is used exclusively for religious purposes or for social welfare, such as the building of hospitals or schools. In other societies, people are responsible themselves for making the charitable contributions to causes of their choice. Some Muslims give the entire sum to their local mosque or to a respected religious leader, who applies it to good use. This practice is particularly common among Shi'is and is partly responsible for the greater social influence enjoyed by Shi'i clerical families when compared to their Sunni counterparts. Other Muslims divide the money and give some of it to charities and the rest directly to needy individuals.

> **Bet You Didn't Know**
>
> In the past, wealthy Muslims used their zakat to support poorer families or destitute orphans, for the duration of the recipients' lives. Others endowed entire schools or hospitals and covered their expenses. Such uses of zakat have become uncommon in modern times, but they are not unheard of.

Pilgrimage: Hajj

Hajj is the name of the pilgrimage to Mecca, which all Muslims are supposed to perform once in their lives if they have the means to do so. The Hajj must be undertaken at a specific time of year, from the first few days of the pilgrimage month (the last month of the Islamic calendar, known as Dhu al-hijja) up to the tenth of the same month. If the pilgrimage to Mecca is carried out at some other time of year, and thus does not include an important set of rituals that take place at sacred sites outside the city, it is called an *umra*; it is still a good deed but does not fulfill a Muslim's duty to perform the Hajj.

For 1,400 years, the Hajj has replayed the pilgrimage performed by Muhammad after Mecca had surrendered to the Muslims. Participants enter a state of ritual purity and wear a special pilgrim's dress before arriving in Mecca, and for the entire period of the Hajj abstain from paying attention to their appearance. They begin by walking seven times around the Ka'ba, the focal point of Islamic faith. The Ka'ba is a simple brick building believed to have been built by Abraham as a temple for God and now serves not only as the focus of the Hajj but also as the direction in which Muslims pray, regardless of where in the world they may be.

> **Muslim Meaning**
>
> **Umra** is a pilgrimage to the Ka'ba in Mecca that is carried out at any time of the year except that of the ritually obligatory Hajj. The umra is considered inferior to the Hajj, but still carries religious merit.

After completing their circuits around the Ka'ba, the pilgrims run between two small hills named Safa and Marwa. This ritual recalls an episode in the life of Abraham and his family, in which Abraham had abandoned Hagar and her infant son Ishmael (Isma'il in Arabic) in the desert. When Ishmael cried out in thirst, Hagar ran seven times back and forth between Safa and Marwa looking for water. In the meantime, Ishmael is said to have kicked his heels into the sand, miraculously causing a spring to appear. This spring, called Zamzam, is believed to possess spiritual powers, and pilgrims take its water as souvenirs at the completion of the

Hajj. The water is also frequently used for anointing bodies during funerary rites.

Bet You Didn't Know

In modern times, it takes a feat of organization to enable up to two million pilgrims to perform the same rituals in the same place over a few days. The Saudi Arabian government has invested large sums of money to create pedestrian highways, tunnels, and galleries to make the Hajj work as smoothly as possible. Jiddah airport, which serves Mecca, becomes one of the busiest in the world during the days immediately before and after the Hajj. Despite the best intentions of the authorities, accidents are not uncommon, and overcrowding sometimes results in large numbers of casualties.

After completing the rounds between the two hills, the Hajj pilgrims then travel to two towns near Mecca to commemorate other events in the life of Abraham. The last part of the Hajj involves spending an afternoon in the plain of Arafat, where Muhammad delivered what came to be called his Farewell Sermon. The Hajj comes to an end on the third day, when the pilgrims sacrifice sheep and goats (and occasionally bulls and camels) in memory of Abraham's willingness to sacrifice his son and God's substitution of a ram in his stead. This sacrifice ends the Hajj and the pilgrims are free to resume their regular dress and grooming.

Before the advent of air travel and modern shipping, the Hajj was an arduous undertaking that required a great deal of preparation. The slowness of the journey and dangers involved also meant that pilgrims had to settle their affairs and make provisions for their families because of the genuine possibility that they might never return. For these reasons, the departure of the Hajj caravans was a major event in all Islamic towns, and remains so to this day.

Jihad

Jihad, which means "striving in the path of God," is one of the most misinterpreted concepts in Islam. It covers all activities that either defend Islam or else further its cause. As such, wars in which Muslims tried to bring new lands under Islam were known as Jihad wars, and were understood and justified by Muslims in a way similar to that in which Christians understood the Crusades. Like the concept of crusades, this meaning of Jihad is mostly irrelevant today.

In modern times, any war that is viewed as a defense of one's own country, home, or community is called a Jihad. This understanding is very similar to what is called "just war" in Western society. In similar fashion, political extremists who believe their cause is just, often refer to their guerilla or terrorist wars as

Jihad, even when the majority of their own society considers their acts to be completely unjustified. It is important to note that engaging in violent acts that intentionally target civilians or cause environmental destruction are expressly forbidden by the rules of Jihad and are not condoned by Islamic law.

Islamic scholars speak of an outer Jihad, which could be either Jihad of the Sword (meaning "warfare"), or Jihad of the Pen—engaging in written defenses of Islam, missionary activity, or simply furthering one's own education. However, there is also an inner Jihad—the battle that all individuals wage against their own baser instincts. Because of its inherent difficulty, this is often called the Greater Jihad.

The Least You Need to Know

- Shahada is the statement of bearing witness that forms the credal formula of Islam; literally, it translates as: "I bear witness that there is no god except the God and I bear witness that Muhammad is the messenger of God!"

- A human voice rings out the Islamic call to prayer (adhan) five times a day, marking the time for prayer—(salat), which is performed in a prescribed manner.

- Muslims are supposed to fast during the ninth lunar month of Ramadan; the fast consists of abstaining from eating, drinking, smoking, violence, and engaging in sex from before sunrise until after sunset for the entire month.

- Alms-giving (zakat) is differentiated from other forms of donations because it is done ritually, consisting of giving away a certain percentage of one's wealth to charity.

- Hajj is the name of the pilgrimage to Mecca (at a specific time of year), which all Muslims are supposed to perform once in their lives if they have the means to do so.

- Jihad means "striving in the path of God." It means the inner struggle to better oneself as well as any armed struggle in the defense of one's home or faith—similar to the concept of "just war" in Western society. Islamic law expressly forbids violent acts targeting civilians or causing destruction to the environment.

Chapter **8**

Islamic Thought in the Modern World

In This Chapter

- Islam expands and contracts
- Fundamentalists and Traditionalists and Islamists, oh my!
- Ayatollah Khomeini and Ali Shari'ati

The desire to strengthen Islam from within and simultaneously to defend it from the perceived onslaught of the West has dominated much of Islamic thought in the last century, and has shaped the attitudes of a wide range of Islamic groups. Muslim reformers of many types, but particularly the Islamists, are trapped between two obstacles—not only do they feel threatened by the Western world, but they are also weighted down by the memory of their own glorious past. This chapter will cover Islamic thought from tradition to reform and give a brief description of some of the most influential Muslim thinkers.

The Fall of Baghdad and the Rise of Europe

The Islamic world continued to expand geographically, culturally, and politically throughout the centuries of Abbasid dominance and even after that empire's political decline in the twelfth and thirteenth centuries. The first half of the thirteenth century was a critical time in Islamic history because of the Mongol invasion, which spread across western Asia and culminated in the destruction of the imperial capital of Baghdad in 1258.

Baghdad was the Rome of its day: It was the seat of the Abbasids, the central city of the Islamic world, and in many ways it was the most cosmopolitan city in the Mediterranean world. Its destruction and the accompanying subjugation of the important Islamic regions of Iran and Iraq to non-Muslim Mongol rule were a major crisis in Muslims' perception of themselves as God's favored religious community. This, in turn, created a theological trauma unmatched by any other until the advent of European colonialism.

Mongol rule proved to be extremely short-lived, but it heralded a new era in which cultural and political dominance in the Islamic world shifted away from Arabs toward Persians, Turks, and other ethnic groups. However, Arabic continued to be the language of most scholarship and also of communications between people from far-flung regions of the Islamic world. Throughout this period, missionaries, mystics, and merchants carried Islam farther abroad, so that by the sixteenth century it had become established in Indonesia, East Africa, and the grasslands south of the Sahara in West Africa.

Islam reached its maximum social and geographic expansion in the seventeenth century, at about the same time that Europe began to make rapid political and cultural gains. Many observers have seen a causal relationship between the declining power and importance of the Islamic world and the rise of Christian Europe. Muslim historical revisionists blame the shift in power on the intellectual stagnation of Muslim scholars, who are accused of ceasing to be intellectually innovative from as early as the thirteenth century, when there was a proverbial closing of the doors of *ijtihad* (independent reasoning).

Europeans have wanted to see this as a result of the genius of their civilization as epitomized in the Renaissance and the Enlightenment. Apart from these broader societal changes, rapid technological advancements undoubtedly helped the West. For instance, superior naval technology enabled European nations to "discover" the Americas. It was not long before access to new sources of gold and trade propelled European development so swiftly that, in comparison, Islamic and Chinese cultures appeared to be standing still.

Islam in the Colonial Age

The encounter with Europe through colonialism and the unquestionable economic and military dominance of the world by the West in the postcolonial period have been critical in the development of Islam. With the exception of Turkey, Iran, Afghanistan, and Saudi Arabia, all Islamic countries were once under colonial rule. Even those that were not formally colonies did not escape the shadow of colonialism:

- Saudi Arabia, Iran, and Afghanistan were protectorates or else had to make substantial concessions in sovereignty to the British or the Russians.

- Turkey, the central province of the Ottoman Empire, was in constant contact with western European powers through its territories in Eastern Europe and North Africa, and had to make humiliating concessions to them in the nineteenth and early twentieth centuries.

In the nineteenth century, many Muslims acknowledged that the European world had attained a level of technology and scientific knowledge that far surpassed anything found in the Islamic world. Many members of the intellectual and political elite felt that the Islamic world needed to modernize its educational and state institutions in order to compete favorably with the West. The Ottoman Empire, in many ways the guardian of Islamic traditionalism, began a process of reform that eventually led to the emergence of Turkey as a secular republic. A ministry was established to administer religious endowments and trusts that previously had been independent. In 1868, the first European-style school opened in Istanbul, and an Ottoman parliament was established in 1876.

Tradition and Reform

Muslim thinkers of the eighteenth and nineteenth centuries have, for the most part, been preoccupied with the problem of strengthening and bettering their communities. Whether they see this as revitalization or simply as vitalization depends on their view of the Islamic past and its relationship to the future. Some thinkers adopt a developmental view, which sees societal progress as contingent upon the adoption of a rationalistic, scientific worldview.

Recent Muslim scholars, however, have tended to drop this model as too materialistic. In their opinion, it simply disregards the context in which development is supposed to occur. They prefer to emphasize "authenticity," which better encapsulates society's distinctive needs. In an Islamic context, authenticity can take one of two forms:

- Individual authenticity, in which individual Muslims should seek to perfect themselves.

- Collective authenticity, wherein Muslims should strive to create a community that lives up to the full potential ordained for it by God.

The notion of authenticity dominates much of Islamic thinking, covering a spectrum ranging from extremely esoteric notions of individual spiritual perfection of the spiritual model to socially active movements that see Islamic authenticity as a society purged of all Western influences. In all cases, the quest for authenticity is based in a belief that there is an ideal form of Islam that is embodied either literally or metaphorically in the Qur'an and in the life of the Prophet. This "authentic" Islam is attainable and is the sole way of vitalizing Islam and individual Muslims.

The Fundamentalists

Western commentators have labeled an entire spectrum of Islamic movements and individual figures as fundamentalist, and the term has attained wide currency in discussions about Islam in the contemporary world. There can be no doubt that there are Muslim fundamentalists, inasmuch as fundamentalism is defined as the belief in the following:

- The infallibility of scripture
- Scripture's literal truth and applicability across time and space
- The existence of an ideal form of the religion that would endure, regardless of whether or not there were people actually practicing it at a specific point in time
- The existence of an ideal or utopian religious community some time in the past

But since belief in the Qur'an as God's literal and eternal word is central to Islam, one could argue that the majority of Muslims are, in fact, fundamentalists. For this reason alone, "fundamentalism" is not a satisfactory term to use in understanding categories of thought in the Islamic world. Yet, other terms—reformism, revivalism, radicalism, and so on—are also not employed consistently, and can be equally misleading.

The Traditionalists

Traditionalists are those Muslims who see a continuity in Islamic thought and culture from the Prophet's day forward, until the fabric of Islamic society was damaged by European colonialism. They would like to see a return to pre-colonial times and the "authentic" Islamic society of that age, represented by traditional Islamic educational and social institutions, systems of government, and religious hierarchies.

At its extreme, traditionalism rejects technological advances in their entirety, including electricity, modern medicine, and railroads (as was the case with the *Wahhabi* movement in Saudi Arabia in the early part of the twentieth century, although they have now come to accept technological development). Traditionalism is largely a defunct ideology, and is normally associated with aging religious scholars who see the modern world as undermining the privileges enjoyed by their profession.

> **Muslim Meaning**
>
> **Wahhabism** is a traditionalist Islamic movement, concentrated in Saudi Arabia that sees modern technological and social innovations as corrupt, and advocates a return to a Muslim society similar to the one in the days of the Prophet.

The Islamists

Juxtaposed to traditionalists are not just modernists but a much wider category of moderns. An important variety of moderns are the Islamists, individuals who believe in the necessity of establishing a society based on Islamic principles and governed by their own understanding of Islamic law and values.

Most Islamists believe that by implementing Islamic law and "enjoining the good and forbidding the evil" they can convince the citizens of the state to adopt "authentic" Islamic values and practices, thereby creating an authentic Islamic society. It is essential to note that Islamists are not modernists, but they are certainly moderns in that they are conscious and active participants in the modern world, for example, in the rapid social transformations that are occurring in the Muslim world through urbanization and migration, or in the use of the modern world's tools—ranging from the cars that have revolutionized transportation to the computers that have radically simplified information-sharing through print media and cyberspace.

Modernists, by contrast, subscribe to a spectrum of ideologies, all of which are united in their acknowledgment of a new significance to the nature of human life, characterized by particular forms of rational thinking and by a belief in the importance of the individual. They tend to share the belief that the processes leading up to the modern era involve a radical shift from traditional values, in which modern scientific and rational thinking replaces beliefs based on faith.

In simplistic terms, Islamists embrace technology, while modernists embrace the systems of values and thought that generate technology. Many Muslim modernists, particularly those from the end of the nineteenth and first half of the twentieth centuries, were deeply impressed by the accomplishments of modern science and held a deep optimism for the promises implicit within the scientific method. More recent modernists have, like many non-Muslim thinkers, developed a sober attitude toward industrial and capitalist development and their negative side-effects, and have embraced attitudes that center on individual rather than societal development.

Many Muslim modernists also embrace the ideology of *liberalism*, particularly in regard to the differentiation between opinion and truth, and the consequent belief that individuals holding different opinions can engage in debate. As a consequence of such debate, one might be able to convince others of the value of one's own opinion, just as one might be convinced that the other's opinion is superior. As a matter of course, Islamists are not liberals, in that they do not allow for the possibility that there might be a difference between their personal idea of what is true and what is actually true.

> **Muslim Meaning**
>
> **Liberalism** is an ideology that emphasizes, among other things, the difference between opinion and truth; it is based on the belief that people or groups with differing views should engage each other in dialogue rather than try to prevail over weaker ones through violent or oppressive means.

The Iranian Revolution

Twelver Shi'ism became the majority religion in Iran (classical Persia) from the 1600s, but this posed an ironic dilemma for its clerics. Historically, Shi'ism represented the oppressed, not the powerful; and doctrinally, Shi'ism considered that all governments would inevitably be corrupt until the hidden Imam returned to redeem humanity. Either way, politics was seen as a "dirty business," and political activism was thought to be futile.

Yet, equally logically, these same beliefs fostered a strong, independent religious hierarchy. In fact, this trend was accentuated in the eighteenth century, when a brief Sunni Afghan occupation of Iran forced Iranian Shi'i scholars to flee to Ottoman-ruled Iraq. There, in the cities of Najaf and Karbala, near the tombs of Ali and Husayn, senior clerics called *Ayatollahs* lived and studied. Even after Shi'is recovered the Iranian throne, most Ayatollahs remained in Iraq and continued to operate well beyond the reach of the Iranian state.

Taken together, these factors help to explain the ability of the Iranian *ulama* (religious scholars) to act independently of and in opposition to the monarchy during the nineteenth and twentieth centuries.

> ### Muslim Meaning
>
> **Ayatollahs** are the high-ranking members of the Twelver Shi'i clergy who are authorized to engage in ijtihad (independent reasoning).

In 1921, a brigadier-general overthrew the ruling Iranian dynasty, and with the blessing of the traditionalist clergy, he crowned himself king in December 1925. In succeeding years, his artificially created Pahlavi dynasty (so named for its mythological pre-Islamic resonances) used the clergy as a foil against modernists, who demanded a more democratic system of government. The clerics disliked his pro-Western policies and monarchial pretensions, but acquiesced in the arrangement, preferring Pahlavi rule to the nightmare of a communist regime (a real fear, given the long border Iran shared with the Soviet Union).

However, by the 1960s, Iran's human-rights abuses and its overly conciliatory policies toward the United States led to anti-government demonstrations, involving both clerics and liberal elements. Ayatollah

Khomeini emerged as the regime's most outspoken critic, and he was arrested after government forces attacked his seminary in Qom. Thousands died in rioting against his imprisonment. In 1964, an unrepentant Khomeini was exiled first to Iraq and then to France, from where he continued his campaign of denunciation.

Finally, in 1978, a wide coalition of secularist and religious intellectuals, trade unionists, communists, and women's groups forced the Shah to leave Iran. But when clerics established a fully fledged "Islamic republic" in 1979, many participants in the struggle against the Shah felt cheated. Not only were they not represented in the new government, but the new regime employed the same security machinery and committed the same atrocities as the Shah did, in order to silence all opposition.

Ayatollah Khomeini

Ayatollah Khomeini (1902–1989) claimed that it was the duty of religious scholars to bring about an Islamic state and to assume legislative, executive, and judicial positions within it. This particular form of government was to be referred to as "Rule of the Jurisprudent" (*velayat-e faqih*). The highest authority was to be a religious scholar who held absolute executive power, and who was qualified to hold this office on the basis of unrivaled knowledge of religious law. He was meant to have such a high level of moral excellence that he was, in fact, untainted by any major sin. There can be little doubt that when Ayatollah Khomeini took over as the religious leader of Iran after the Islamic Revolution, he was ruling in precisely this capacity.

Khomeini based his ideas of governance by scholars on Islamic precedents, including the hadith, which said: "The scholars of my community are like the prophets before me." Khomeini shared the idea that virtuous leadership creates a virtuous society with other Islamists. However, unlike most other Islamists of the twentieth century, he also stressed the symbolism of class and economic exploitation, which resonated with Marxist opponents of the Shah. As he put it: "If the ulama … were to implement God's ordinances … the people would no longer be hungry and wretched, and the laws of Islam would no longer be in abeyance."

Bet You Didn't Know

Many of the ideas Khomeini espoused before he became the leader of a revolutionary government are among the most compelling examples of radical Islamist writing and bear a striking resemblance to some of the concepts espoused by advocates of Liberation Theology in Latin America.

Ali Shari'ati

Some scholars have argued that Khomeini's blend of traditional Islamic concern for the poor and the oppressed with Marxist and socialist ideas and symbols was a conscious attempt to capitalize on the enormous popularity of another important Iranian thinker, Ali Shari'ati (1933–1977). Unlike Khomeini, Shari'ati did not belong to a clerical family (although he had received a formal religious education alongside his regular schooling).

After five years of studying in Paris, Shari'ati returned to Iran, but his criticisms of the Shah resulted in his expulsion back to France, where he died in what many regard as suspicious circumstances. Shari'ati lamented the fact that the best scholarship on Islam was conducted by Europeans and not by Muslims themselves. "As the followers of a great religion, [we must] learn and know Islam correctly and methodically. The mere holding of a belief is no virtue in itself," he said.

Shari'ati exhorted his audience to become authentic by discovering their individual uniqueness. His works repeatedly explore this theme, using the example of Shi'i heroes like Fatima, Muhammad's daughter, who transcends her societal role to fulfill her destiny as a consummate human being.

Shari'ati saw the overarching message of Shi'i Islam as being a struggle to improve society through self-sacrifice. In this regard, he quoted the example of Husayn, Fatima's son, who voluntarily accepted martyrdom in order to expose the criminal nature of his "evil enemies." Shari'ati wrote: "Shahadat (martyrdom) is an invitation to all generations, in all ages, [that] if you cannot kill your oppressor, then die." In Arabic, the term shahadat connotes both martyrdom and bearing witness. What, then, is made of the person who commits shahadat but remains alive to bear witness? To Shari'ati, this sort of person—epitomized by Husayn's sister, Zaynab—had the special role of reminding the community of its individual and collective religious duties.

Final "Thought" on the Thinkers

The thinkers presented here represent a variety of viewpoints that have proved influential in the last century. A clear progression can be traced from the early modernists to those who are influential today.

These thinkers stand in contrast to the Islamists who actively agitate for an Islamic order enforced through the power of the state. As is apparent from the example of Khomeini, many Islamists have been heavily influenced by the ideas of Muslim modernists, although they are selective in what they accept, and reject most liberal ideas.

This trend continues to be present, breeding a high level of distrust between individuals who have differing ideas regarding the future of Islam and Muslims.

The Least You Need to Know

- Islam reached its maximum social and geographic expansion in the seventeenth century at about the same time as Europe began to make rapid political and cultural gains.

- Modernist Muslims see great potential for improving Islamic societies through embracing science and industrialization. They focus on promoting liberal values inherent in European notions of modernism.

- Traditionalists are those Muslims who see a continuity in Islamic thought and culture from the Prophet's day forward; they would like to see a return to the "authentic" Islamic society represented by traditional Islamic educational and social institutions, systems of government, and religious hierarchies.

- Most Islamist Muslims believe that by implementing Islamic law they can convince the citizens of the state to adopt "authentic" Islamic values and practices. They believe that virtuous leadership creates a virtuous society.

Looking to the Future

In This Chapter

- History goes on
- September 11 and the Islamic world
- Women's role within Islam
- Where will Islam go from here?

Many Muslims remain acutely conscious of their glorious past, when the Islamic world was home to many of the world's richest cities and most important centers of learning. They find it impossible to reconcile their perception of their own destiny as a beacon to the rest of humanity with the fact that, at present, they are in no position to compete favorably with other, more vital societies, as well as with the bitter fact that no Muslim country ranked among the most developed nations. This chapter talks about some of the recent hot topics that surround the Islamic faith and that Muslims consider as they look toward the future.

The Muslim Worldview

Islam is a religion with over one billion adherents worldwide, with established populations on every inhabited continent of the planet. Within 100 years of its emergence in the Arabian peninsula in the seventh century C.E., Muslim communities could be found living in Asia, Africa, and Europe.

A remarkable feature of Islamic history is that, with only one significant exception, all lands to which Islam spread among the population have remained Muslim into modern times. The exception is Spain and Portugal, where the long process of Christian reconquest (called the Reconquista), followed by the Spanish Inquisition, systematically eradicated the area's Muslim population. Even so, when the edict for the final expulsion of Muslims and Jews was issued (127 years after the end of the Reconquista in 1492), around two million Muslims fled the kingdom of Castile alone, giving some indication of the degree to which Islam had been integrated into Spanish life.

Islam continues to be the majority religion in countries as diverse as Morocco in the west and Indonesia in the east, and from Senegal in the south to Kazakhstan in the north. In each of these countries, Islam is practiced in a distinct way, the differences being most apparent in the way people dress and in the customs surrounding such life-events as birth and marriage. Thus, Bosnian Muslims live their lives in ways that have more in common with their Christian neighbors than with the Muslims of Pakistan, and the Muslims of Indonesia have incorporated many elements of Hindu mythology into their religious lives.

In other places, local Muslim customs reflect the need to set the Muslims off from their non-Muslim neighbors. For example, Indian Muslims eat particular foods and avoid certain colors and flowers in their weddings for the specific purpose of maintaining their differences from the Hindu majority. It is therefore possible to speak of numerous "fault-lines" of identity along which one can differentiate Muslims, these being lines of language, ethnicity, race, nationhood, gender, attitudes toward the modern world, experience with colonialism, age, economic status, social status, sectarian identity, and so on. Any statement about Muslim beliefs that claims to be universal inevitably ends up being disproved by exceptions somewhere else in the Muslim world.

Nonetheless, the majority of Muslims retain a remarkable similarity in their rituals, a fact that is reinforced by the almost universal use of Arabic as the language of prayer and liturgy. Furthermore, even though Muslims have as highly developed sense of nationalism and patriotism as anyone else, many of them retain the sense that they all belong to one community. For this reason, the Muslim citizens of a particular region or country will greet fellow Muslims from distant, unrelated societies with a warmth and a sense of kinship that is very rare in most other religious communities.

> **On the Right Path**
>
> Even though some Muslims, particularly those with an extremely politicized understanding of Islam, will criticize other Muslims to the point of considering them nonbelievers or apostates (individuals who have renounced their faith), when the Muslims of whom they are critical are faced with an external threat (as in Chechnya or Bosnia), the first group will frequently suspend its criticism and extend the umbrella of its sympathy and aid to the Muslims in need of support.

Muslim Minorities in the West

There is ample evidence that Muslims in the United States, Britain, France, and other countries are consciously mastering the symbols and tools of Western society (television and print media, and, increasingly, the Internet)—because they believe that these skills will both strengthen the Muslim community internally and help Muslims to gain greater visibility and voice in the societies in which they live as minorities.

It is, in fact, largely through the efforts of such individuals, and not the assimilated elites, that Muslims have gained social recognition in Europe and North America.

At the same time as the British Home Office was warning that police attitudes toward the large community of Pakistani and Bangladeshi immigrants have created suspicion and hostility among these minorities and could lead to ethnic riots, in 1997 Britain elected its first Muslim member of Parliament, and in 1998 the Ministry of Education approved two Islamic schools, one in London and the other in Birmingham, for inclusion among state-funded institutions. With this decision, Islamic religious schools and the education they impart are now beginning to attain a status commensurate with that enjoyed by schools run by the Church of England, the Roman Catholic Church, and the Jewish community.

The case of the United States is somewhat different because of Islam's stature as an important religion among African Americans who are viewed as more "authentic" Americans than are members of the immigrant community. Islam came to the Americas with the first slaves brought over from West Africa. Though actively suppressed to the point of extinction under slavery, Islam gained a new symbolic importance in the United States during the Civil Rights Era, when it was identified as authentically African, as distinct from Christianity, which was seen as a "White Religion."

Although early groups, such as the Moorish Science Temple and the Nation of Islam under Elijah Muhammad, were viewed as not quite Muslim by immigrants, under the leadership of Warith Deen Muhammad (and the posthumous charismatic influence of Malcolm X), the overwhelming majority of

African American Muslims have assimilated to Sunni Islam. A smaller group follows the Nation of Islam of Louis Farrakhan, but they are not considered Muslims by the majority.

Cooperation between African American and immigrant Muslims—who together number approximately five million people—has resulted in a number of substantive changes for the betterment of Islam's status in the United States. For example, in the 1990s, the U.S. president started issuing statements on major Islamic religious holidays, sessions of Congress were opened with Muslim prayers, and the U.S. military admitted Muslim chaplains.

September 11 and Muslims

One of the toughest challenges faced by the majority of Muslims today is the rise of small, extremist groups that engage in political violence—or terrorism—and justify it in terms of Islam. The most notorious act of violence of this nature was perpetrated on September 11, 2001, by a shadowy group named Al-Qaeda. International scrutiny following those attacks exposed the existence of a nebulous, largely underground network of groups committed to achieving their ends through violent means.

It is important to note that extremist groups of this nature commit the majority of their violence against other Muslims, not against the Western world. They engage in sectarian killings and attack mosques, religious gatherings, and schools in many parts of the Islamic world. They frequently believe that their ends justify their means, and therefore are willing to target civilians. They also consider Muslims who do not agree with their agenda to be heretics or apostates, and therefore believe their deaths to be justified.

Bet You Didn't Know

No traditional notion of Islamic law and its rules of warfare or governing societies justifies or even condones acts of terror. The rules covering Jihad in its meaning as "just war" explicitly forbid the killing of Muslims, the intentional targeting of civilians, engaging in disproportionate acts of violence, and giving one's own life in a situation where there is no reasonable expectation of victory. Equally importantly, Islamic law has traditionally taken an extremely harsh view of anyone who violently disrupts the harmony of society. Highway robbery, piracy, and raiding were among the few crimes for which Shari'a law mandated the death penalty. Many Muslim religious scholars today feel that terrorism and hijacking fall under the same rules and should be dealt with as harshly.

Many extremist groups believe that Muslims, as a whole, have gone astray; they feel the only way for them to gain power and establish a virtuous society is through violent means. Many of these groups have a very direct and literal sense that the whole purpose of life is to attain rewards in heaven. As such, traditional Islamic notions of social relationships, charity, care for the needy, and so on have little value in their political agendas.

Extremism of this kind is fed by the current political situation in which most Islamic societies are ruled by governments that are perceived as corrupt and self-serving. Many Muslims, not just extremists, feel that they are deprived of the fruits of their labor and the wealth (such as oil) of their land, and that a disproportionate share of global resources is consumed by the West. They feel that their own governments—especially those of oil-rich countries— are servants of the West, and that they oppress their own people for personal gain. Thus, when extremist groups fight against illegitimate governments and an exploitative world order, they gain the admiration of many people across the Islamic world who feel that the extremists are fighting for them. What they hear in the extremists' message is the claim to represent authentic Islam and the fight for justice and dignity, not the religiously unjustifiable violence the extremists perpetrate.

Islam in Context

A major tension within various Muslim communities is over who represents the normative or authentic form of Islam, and how (if at all) traditional Islamic practices, beliefs, and institutions should be modified to suit a rapidly changing world. Some modernist

Muslims and Western critics tend to see traditional Islamic interpretations of the religion as intolerant and as aggressive threats to the entire enterprise of human progress. They identify Islamic legal and ritual traditions with this backwardness, and either reject Islam entirely or else search for some aspect of the religion that can be made to fit the perceived needs of the contemporary world.

Many commentators on Islam, both Muslim and non-Muslim, try to see a more desirable and tolerant Islamic face in Sufi movements. By contrast, Islamists and traditionalists are sometimes lumped together as conservatives of a bad kind. They are viewed as more concerned with conformity to outdated religious ritual and law than with the spiritual and physical welfare of individuals whom they force to conform to their own notions of acceptable social and religious behavior.

Commentators favoring the Sufi approach identify Islam's traditions of tolerance of behavior and belief as its most desirable feature. The most common barometers of this attitude are the positions concerning women's choices in dress and movement, and whether or not supposedly Islamic values are enforced across a society (for example, restrictions being placed on the public consumption of food during the month of fasting, or on the sale and consumption of alcohol throughout the year). In fact, the correlation between social tolerance and Sufi Islamic societies or systems of authority is not that simple. Many Islamic reformers have specifically targeted problems within Sufism and have successfully exploited negative public perceptions of aspects of Sufistic Islam in order to gain social influence.

Some of the Muslim attacks against Sufism and Sufistic fit within the framework of the desire to spread an "authentic" form of Islam. In the opinion of many reformers, the majority of Sufi beliefs and practices did not exist at the time of Muhammad and are therefore undesirable innovations. Traditionalist Muslims not only criticize much of Sufi philosophy and many practices of meditation, but also reject the expressions of Sufism, which are seen as morally degenerate and hedonistic.

However, a much more potent critique of Sufism society is based on the rigid and exploitative social system that allegiance to hereditary saints actually creates. In some regions of the Islamic world, such as among the Kurds of Turkey and Iraq, the Sindhis of Pakistan, and across parts of Morocco, political power rests with families of hereditary saints, who rely on their reputation as the possessors of baraka (a miraculous power that is bestowed on human beings by God), which functions as a supernatural threat as much as it does a blessing to ensure the loyalty of the local population.

Despite the potential for exploitation inherent in Sufi social structures, in some parts of the Muslim world, people identify Sufism as their genuine, indigenous form of Islam, as distinct from the imported, so-called normative tradition represented by the Islamists. This is particularly true in parts of the former Soviet Union, such as Chechnya, where the population has drawn a distinction between its own traditional form of Islam, which is based on Sufi orders closely tied to clan-based loyalties, and the Wahhabi reformism that is being spread by a network of missionaries allegedly subsidized by Saudi Arabia.

The Wahhabis, who are easily identified by their voluntary adoption of beards, skullcaps, and veils, and their shunning of tribal loyalties in favor of religious ones, are seen by other Chechens as a threat to the traditional way of life and as the vanguard of a new, intolerant form of Islam such as the one enforced in Afghanistan by the Taliban. The Chechen Wahhabis are also seen as better equipped and more violent in their bid to take control of Chechnya.

Many critical universal issues influence this debate in Chechnya: the relationship between common people and elites, among different Muslim societies as well as between Muslim societies and the West, and gender relationships and the role of women. Yet, ultimately the central question is this: Who can claim to embody "authentic" Islam?

Women in Islam

The Qur'an and Hadith literature make extensive references to the status of women, both in terms of their religious and spiritual rights and obligations, and concerning their role and status in society. The general thrust of the Qur'an appears to be to regularize the status of women, which varied enormously within pre-Islamic Arab society. At that time, some people were so displeased with the birth of daughters that they killed them, a practice strongly condemned in the Qur'an:

> When news is brought to one of them, of [the birth of] a female child, his face darkens, and he is filled with inward grief! With shame does he hide himself from his people, because of the bad news he has had! Shall he retain her in contempt, or bury her in the dust? Ah! What an evil they decide on! (16:58–59)

Several other verses in the Qur'an clearly teach that men and women have equal religious rights and responsibilities:

> For Muslim men and women … for men and women who humble themselves; for men and women who give in charity, for men and women who fast, for men and women who guard their chastity, and for men and women who engage much in God's praise, for them has God prepared forgiveness and great reward. (33:35)

Other verses imply biological equality between genders—"[God] created for you mates from among yourselves …" (30:21). The Qur'an also stresses the importance of bonds of affection ("And he has put love and mercy between you" (30:35) and mutual support ("Men and women are protectors, one of another" (9:71)). In other places in the Qur'an, however, men are clearly depicted as superior to women:

> Men are the protectors and maintainers of women because Allah has given the one more than the other, and because they support them from their means. Therefore, the righteous women are devoutly obedient, and guard in [the husband's] absence what God would have them guard. As to those women on whose part you fear disloyalty and ill-conduct, admonish them and banish them to beds apart, and strike them. Then if they obey you, seek not a way against them. Lo! God is most high, great. (4:34)

Many Muslim feminists have argued that verses that endorse the concept of male superiority were included in the Qur'an only because the notion of women's inferiority was so deeply ingrained within Arab society at that time. They blame the patriarchal structure of most Muslim societies on the environments in which Islam spread. In particular, they identify the Mediterranean world as one with a severely misogynistic underpinning, one that was appropriated by Muslims as they spread into cultures that were materially much more advanced than the Arab one and were therefore seen as worthy of imitation. Even the historical development of the Hadith tradition is seen as illustrating this trend. Earlier collections relied heavily on information provided by Muhammad's widow, A'isha, and generally promoted equality between genders. Later collections, however, played down A'isha's role and contained rulings that restrict women's freedoms.

Despite the gender inequalities seen in the majority of Islamic societies, women from all backgrounds usually embrace rather than reject their religious tradition. Muslim feminists refuse to grant legitimacy either to Western critics who see Islam as inherently prejudiced against women, or to Muslim traditionalists who feel that in an Islamic society women should be subordinate to men.

Such women (and men) detect two competing understandings within Islam, one expressed in the pragmatic regulations for society, the other in the articulation of an ethical and moral vision according to which men and women are equal in the eyes of God.

A challenge to Western notions of women's emancipation (which are shared by many Muslim modernists) is posed by a tendency among young professional women to adopt the veil voluntarily as a symbol of their own empowerment. Such women see themselves as striving toward an ideal of authentic Islamic womanhood, and view other women who embrace Western standards of dress and appearance (and who are often the mothers of the newly veiled) as enslaved by value systems that view women as ornaments and playthings.

A Question of Interpretation

Central to most Muslim feminist positions, be they Islamists or modernists, is the belief that certain portions of the Qur'an, which seem to be unequivocal in stating that women are subservient to men, must be read metaphorically and seen as relevant only to the circumstances under which they were revealed.

In arguing for a contextual and metaphorical reading of the Qur'an, Muslim feminists are running counter to the widespread Muslim belief that the Qur'an is literally the word of God and therefore eternally binding in all contexts. However, they are by no means unique in distinguishing between the literal word of the text and its ethical vision.

Many conservative Islamists and traditionalists routinely make such distinctions. A dramatic example is found in debates that occurred in the late 1970s in Pakistan over the religious legitimacy of that country's ban on slavery. Literalists argued that the Qur'anic verse that states that it is a virtuous act to free slaves means that slavery cannot be abolished, since to do so would be to deny future generations the opportunity to commit the virtuous deed of freeing slaves. This reading was resoundingly opposed by a broad spectrum of religious scholars, who read this verse in light of the Qur'an's ethical stand in favor of equality between human beings; they would see the verse as contextual, revealed at a time when Muslims owned slaves, moving them toward a time when they would no longer do so.

A similar tendency toward metaphorical interpretation is found in some Islamists' reading of the Qur'anic verse, cited previously, which allows men to strike their wives. Apologists argue that the striking can be done with something as benign as a feather, stating unequivocally that physical abuse is contrary to Islamic values. However, such an interpretation in no way detracts from the fact that any instance that allows a husband to discipline his wife, but does not allow for the opposite, is incompatible with the notion of gender equality. The position does, however, transcend literalist interpretation, and thereby leaves the door open for future debates on the literal applicability of scripture.

The Future Course of Islam

It is impossible to predict the likely course of future events in all the varied societies that together comprise the Muslim world. However, it is safe to say that a major issue to be resolved in the first half of the twenty-first century is whether or not diverse interpretations of the understandings of Islam will be allowed to exist side by side in Islamic society. Liberal Muslim thinkers advocate a broader understanding of Islam, which encompasses all existing variations in belief and practice.

Unfortunately, current social and political trends, not just in Muslim society but in the world at large, might suggest that liberalism is in retreat in most religions and societies; thus the future holds the prospect of greater divergence between conflicting ideas of authentic Islam. There is a dilemma inherent in secular Islamic countries, such as Uzbekistan, Kazakhstan, and Turkey, which persecute Islamists and deny them rights of political and social expression. Such persecution backfires on the governments in question because it legitimizes the Islamists in the eyes of the populace and lends greater credibility to their allegations that the governments are corrupt and not interested in serving the needs of the people. On the other hand, the existing track record of Islamist groups in a number of societies should give no reason for optimism about their capacity to formulate more competent or ethical governments, or their commitment to preserve the civil and democratic political institutions that they exploit very skillfully in order to gain political power.

On the Right Path

The identification in the public imagination of Islamists the world over with extremist groups such as the Taliban in Afghanistan (linked to Osama bin Laden and the bombing of the World Trade Center in New York City, September 11, 2001,) or the Armed Islamic Group (held responsible for the shocking atrocities in Algeria) weakens the Islamist position and encourages people to think more clearly about the difference between the Islam of their own contexts and the foreign Islam represented by the Islamists.

Perhaps the largest failing of many of the mainstream Islamists and some modernists is that they try to present Islam wholly rationally. Seen from such perspectives, Islam is the ideal religion because (they claim) it has the most efficient legal and social system, or because (in their opinions) it is in complete harmony with science, its truths confirmed by modern scientific discoveries. Such an understanding of Islam has virtually no appeal to the average Muslim—it is also potentially counterproductive because it ends up secularizing the religion by reducing it to nothing more than a legal and political system, albeit a perfect one.

This robs it of any supernatural, sacred, or emotional dimension, precisely that aspect of the religion that inspires human beings not only to hold fast to the rope of faith but also to unfurl the sails of imagination and genius and produce those artistic and intellectual artifacts that are the essence of any civilization. In this respect, it is possible that the future of Islam lies in a renewed appreciation for and examination of its rich heritage, and an embracing of the various modern expressions of this vast and vibrant religion.

The Least You Need to Know

- The majority of Muslims retain a remarkable similarity in their rituals, a fact that is reinforced by the almost universal use of Arabic as the language of prayer and liturgy.

- Most Muslim feminists believe that the Qur'an clearly advocates an ethical and moral equality between men and women, and that inequalities that exist in society are a result of history and culture.

- Religious extremists who engage in acts of terrorism target other Muslims more often than they target the West. No traditional notion of Islamic law and its rules of warfare or governing societies justifies or even condones the actions of such groups.

- A major tension within various Muslim communities is over who represents the normative form of Islam, and how (if at all) traditional Islamic practices, beliefs, and institutions should be modified to suit a rapidly changing world.

Glossary

Abbasids The name of the Sunni dynasty that ruled much of the Islamic world through what has come to be called the Golden Age of Islam.

Abd al Muttalib The name of Muhammad's paternal grandfather.

Abdallah The name of Muhammad's father.

Abu Bakr Muhammad's friend, advisor, father of his wife A'isha, and the first Caliph of the Sunnis.

Abu Talib The name of Muhammad's paternal uncle, who took over his guardianship after he had been orphaned.

adhan (or azan) The Islamic call to prayer that is broadcast from mosques five times a day.

A'isha The name of Abu Bakr's daughter and the wife of Muhammad; she outlived him by several decades and is one of the most important sources of doctrinal and historical information in the formative period of Islam.

al-Ash'ari   The name of the most famous theologian in the history of Islam, and founder of the Ash'ariya school of theology.

al-Azhar   The name of the most prestigious center of Sunni learning and one of the world's oldest surviving universities. It is located in Cairo.

Ali   Muhammad's cousin and son-in-law; considered the first Imam by Shi'i Muslims and the fourth Caliph by Sunnis. He is one of the most important figures in early Islam.

Allah   Literally means "the god," the proper name of God in Islam.

Amina   The name of Muhammad's mother.

Ash'ariya   The name of the most influential school of theology in Islam.

aya (plural: ayat)   Literally means "signs of God"; the term used for individual verses of the Qur'an.

Ayatollah   High-ranking members of the Twelver Shi'i clergy who are authorized to engage in ijtihad.

azan   *See* adhan.

baraka (sometimes barkat or bereket)   A miraculous power bestowed on human beings by God, and believed to be possessed by Sufi saints.

batin   A term used in Sufism and esoteric Shi'i thought for the inner, hidden meaning of a text, particularly the Qur'an.

caliphs   The leaders of the Muslim community after Muhammad. It comes from the Arabic word khalifa, which means "representative" or "delegate," implying that the Caliphs did not rule on their own authority but only as the representatives of God and his Prophet.

Chishti   The name of a Sufi order that is extremely popular in South Asia.

dhikr   *See* zikr.

Eid al-Adha   The "Festival of the Sacrifice" that marks the end of the Hajj pilgrimage.

Eid al-Fitr   The festival that commemorates the end of the fast of Ramadan.

fana   A Sufi mystical concept that signifies the annihilation of a person's individuality in the oneness of God.

faqih   A scholar who engages in the theoretical study of Islamic jurisprudence (fiqh).

Fatima   Muhammad's daughter, wife of Ali, and mother of Husayn. She is a focus of devotion in Shi'i Islam.

fatwa   A legal opinion or decree; the answer given by a mufti to a question posed to him.

fiqh   Islamic jurisprudence.

hadith   Traditions or anecdotes concerning the life and sayings of the Prophet Muhammad; used as a religious source of secondary importance to the Qur'an.

hafiz Literally means "guardian"; an honorific title used for someone who knows the Qur'an by heart.

Hajj A pilgrimage to the Ka'ba in Mecca, which constitutes one of the ritual obligations of Islam.

Hanafi Name of one of the four Sunni legal schools.

Hanbali Name of one of the four Sunni legal schools.

Hashim The name of Muhammad's clan.

Hijra The migration of Muhammad and his followers from Mecca to Medina in 622 C.E., which marks the beginning of the Islamic Hijri calendar.

Husayn The younger son of Ali and Fatima, and grandson of the Prophet. His martyrdom at Karbala is a major focus of Shi'i belief and ritual.

ijtihad The independent reasoning of a qualified Islamic legal scholar, referred to as a mujtahid or faqih.

Imam Literally means "leader"; a term used for anyone who leads prayers in a mosque. More important, it is the title of the rightful leader of the Muslim community in the Shi'i sect.

iman Faith.

Islam Literally means "surrender" or "submission"; the name of a monotheistic religion closely related to Judaism and Christianity; people belonging to this religion are called Muslims.

Islamists   Individuals who believe in the necessity of establishing a society based on Islamic principles and governed by their own understanding of Islamic law and values.

Isma'ilis   The name of a Shi'i sect.

isnad   The chain of transmitting authorities of a hadith account.

Jabriya   An early theological school that maintained that humans act entirely by divine compulsion and have absolutely no free will.

Ja'far al-Sadiq   The sixth Imam of the Shi'is, who is credited with founding the principal school of Shi'i law.

Jama'at-e Islami   The most powerful Islamist organization among the Muslims of South Asia, with strong ties to Sunni Islamist organizations all over the world and growing influence in Central Asia.

Jihad   The term literally means "striving" and is a shortened version of a longer name that means "striving in the path of God." The concept of jihad covers all activities that either defend Islam or else further its cause.

jinn   Sentient beings mentioned in the Qur'an, frequently identified as demons.

Ka'ba   A cubic building located in Mecca, believed to have been built by Abraham at God's command. It is the direction in which Muslims pray and is the focus of the ritual pilgrimage called the Hajj.

Kalam Literally means "Speech" or "dialectic"; the most common name given to theology in Islam.

Khadija The name of the Prophet's first wife, who is also honored as the first convert to Islam.

Khalifa *See* Caliph.

Koran *See* Qur'an.

liberalism An ideology that emphasizes, among other things, the difference between opinion and truth; it is based on the belief that people or groups with differing views should engage each other in dialogue rather than try to prevail over weaker ones through violent or oppressive means.

Maliki Name of one of the four Sunni legal schools.

masjid A Muslim place of prayer; same as a mosque.

Mevlevi The name of a Sufi order that is limited to Turkey and some other areas that once belonged to the Ottoman Empire. Famous for its distinctive zikr ritual, called sema.

mihrab A prayer niche in a mosque that marks the qibla, or direction, of prayer.

minbar A pulpit, one of the most important architectural features of a mosque.

modernists Reformists who subscribe to a spectrum of ideologies, all of which are united in their acknowledgment that the modern significances of human life are substantially different from those that came before it. Modernism is characterized by particular forms of rational thinking and by the belief in the importance of the individual.

mosque   A Muslim place of prayer; same as a masjid.

mufti   Someone normally appointed by the government for the specific purpose of answering questions concerning Islamic law (shari'a).

Muhammad   The primary prophet of Islam, believed by Muslims to have received divine revelation in the form of the Qur'an, and to be the last in a series of prophets beginning with Adam and including all the prophets mentioned in the Hebrew Bible, as well as Jesus.

Muharram   The name of the first month of the Islamic calendar, synonymous with a mourning ritual practiced by members of the Twelver Shi'i sect to commemorate the martyrdom of Muhammad's cousin Ali and more important, Ali's son and Muhammad's grandson Husayn.

mujtahid   A respected and learned Muslim scholar who has the right to engage in independent reasoning, or ijtihad.

Muslim (f. Muslima)   A person who professes the religion of Islam.

Muslim Brotherhood (Al-Ikhwan al-muslimin) The most powerful Islamist organization in the Arab world, with strong ties to Sunni Islamist organizations in other Muslim societies.

Mu'tazila   The name of one of the most important and influential theological schools in the history of Islam.

nabi (plural: anbiya) A prophet. Belief in prophecy is an important tenet of Muslim belief.

namaz The name of the Islamic ritual prayer; the same as salat.

Qadariya An early Islamic theological school that believed in absolute human free will.

qadi An Islamic judge.

qawwali A very distinctive form of singing practiced by members of the Chishti Sufi order as part of their dhikr exercises.

qibla The direction of Muslim prayer, which is supposed to be performed facing the Ka'ba in Mecca from all points in the world.

Qur'an The Muslim scripture that is believed to have been revealed by God to the Prophet Muhammad.

Quraysh The name of Muhammad's tribe.

Ramadan The ninth month of the Islamic lunar calendar, during which practicing Muslims fast, abstaining from eating, drinking, smoking, violence, and sex from before sunrise until after sunset for the entire month.

rasul (plural: rusul) A special category of prophet (nabi), to whom God has given a concrete message, normally a revealed scripture, to be delivered to human beings.

sajda The bowing down or prostration that is one of the most distinctive aspects of Islamic ritual prayer or salat.

salat The name of the Islamic ritual prayer; the same as namaz.

sema A very distinctive whirling dance performed by members of the Mevlevi Sufi order as part of their dhikr exercises.

Shafi'i The name of one of the four Sunni legal schools.

Shahada The Islamic profession of faith: "I bear witness that there is no god except the God and I bear witness that Muhammad is the messenger of God!"

Shari'a Islamic law.

Shi'ah Same as Shi'i.

Shi'i The name given to a number of Muslim sects, all of which separated from the Sunni Muslim majority over the status of Ali as the successor to Muhammad.

Shi'ite Same as Shi'i.

Sufism The name given to a wide range of expressions of mystical religiosity in Islam; the same as tasawwuf.

Sunna The custom or tradition of the Prophet Muhammad, which is used as a source of law and as an informal model of behavior in everyday life.

Sunni The name of the majority sect in Islam.

sura The term used for individual chapters of the Qur'an.

Tanzimat A period of modernizing reforms carried out in the Ottoman Empire lasting from 1839 to 1876.

tariqas Sufi orders that have been very important in the history of Islamic thought and society.

tasawwuf The name given to a wide range of expressions of mystical religiosity in Islam; the same as Sufism.

tawhid The concept of divine unity, which is central to Muslim belief.

traditionalists Those Muslims who see a continuity in Islamic thought and culture from the Prophet's day forward, until the fabric of Islamic society was damaged by European colonialism, and who would like to see a return to pre-colonial times.

Twelver Shi'is The name of an important Shi'i sect, which is dominant in Iran.

ulama (singular: alim) The class of Muslim religious scholars.

Umayyads The first dynasty to rule the Islamic world.

umma (ummat) Means "nation" or "community" and refers to the community of believers made up by all the Muslims of the world.

umra A pilgrimage to the Ka'ba in Mecca that is carried out at any time of the year except that of the ritually obligatory Hajj. The umra is considered inferior to the Hajj, but still carries religious merit.

usul al-fiqh   The principles of Islamic jurisprudence, which are used to interpret Islamic law (shari'a).

Wahhabism   A traditionalist Islamic movement, concentrated in Saudi Arabia, which sees modern technological and social innovations as corrupt and agitates for a return to a Muslim society similar to the one in the days of the Prophet.

wudu (or wuzu)   The ritual washing that precedes prayers (salat).

zahir   A term used in Sufism and esoteric Shi'i thought for the outer, obvious meaning of a text, particularly the Qur'an.

zakat   Ritual alms-giving that consists of giving a fixed percentage of one's wealth to charity every year.

Zaydis   The name of a Shi'i sect that is largely limited to Yemen.

zikr   Literally means "repetition," "remembrance," "utterance," or "mentioning," and is the commonest term used for Sufi meditational exercises.

Index

G-H

I

W-X

Y-Z